DATE DUE

MAY 1 5 1991 ENDS		APR 0 4 '91	
		MAY 1 4 1992	
MAY 31 1994 BIRD		JUN 8 1993	

JEAN BODIN AND THE
SIXTEENTH-CENTURY REVOLUTION
IN THE METHODOLOGY OF
LAW AND HISTORY

JEAN BODIN

AND THE
SIXTEENTH-CENTURY
REVOLUTION IN
THE METHODOLOGY OF
LAW AND HISTORY

By JULIAN H. FRANKLIN

ASSOCIATE PROFESSOR OF PUBLIC LAW AND GOVERNMENT

COLUMBIA UNIVERSITY

NEW YORK AND LONDON

COLUMBIA UNIVERSITY PRESS

1963

TO MY PARENTS

This study, prepared under the Graduate Faculties of Columbia University, was selected by a committee of those Faculties to receive one of the Clarke F. Ansley awards given annually by Columbia University Press.

ACKNOWLEDGMENTS

In the preparation and completion of this study I was greatly aided and encouraged by the discerning judgment and warm support of Professor Herbert A. Deane, who was the sponsor of my dissertation. I am grateful also to Professor David B. Truman for his friendly interest and useful comments on the final manuscript. And I am indebted to my readers, Professor Garrett Mattingly and A. Arthur Schiller, as well as to Professors Robert D. Cumming and Neal B. Wood, for their many helpful suggestions. Professor Paul O. Kristeller and Dr. Donald Kelly were also kind enough to read the final manuscript and to suggest additional revisions. And I was greatly helped at all stages of my work by the generous advice and encouragement of my friends, Abraham Ascher, Emanuel S. Chill, Martin Fleisher, Peter J. Gay, Andrew Martin, and Rudolph Weingartner. I should also like to acknowledge here the pervasive influence on all my thought of my former teacher, the late Professor Franz L. Neumann.

In revising this work for publication I was aided by a grant from Princeton University for the summer of 1961. I should also like to express my thanks to Miss Elisabeth Shoemaker of Columbia University Press for her wisdom and patience in helping me to edit the manuscript, to Miss Elizabeth Seid for her help with the typing, and to Mrs.

Joan Levinson and Mr. Mordecai Melnitsky for their aid in the correction of proofs.

In acknowledging these debts of gratitude I am deeply mindful that the errors and omissions which remain are my responsibility alone.

Julian H. Franklin

Columbia University,
November 6, 1962

NOTE

All translations are my own unless otherwise indicated. Although the translations from the Latin works of Jean Bodin are my responsibility, I have occasionally consulted the French version of these works provided by Pierre Mesnard and the English translation of Bodin's *Methodus ad facilem historiarum cognitionem* by Beatrice Reynolds (New York, 1945). I am grateful to the George H. Macy Companies for permission to quote several passages from Jacques LeClercq's translation of Rabelais, *The Five Books of Gargantua and Pantagruel,* and to Cambridge University Press for permission to quote a passage from G. G. Coulton's *Medieval Panorama.*

CONTENTS

INTRODUCTION

The last quarter of the sixteenth century marks a new development in jurisprudence which is of great importance not only for the social sciences but for the theory of history as well. Secular legal science in the later middle ages was almost exclusively focused on exegesis of the Roman Law as it was known from the codification of Justinian. In its actual results this study of the *Corpus Juris* had been a genuinely creative process of adapting Roman concepts to the needs of medieval Europe. But the creative contribution of the medieval jurist had never been reflected in his premise. In principle, at least, the *Corpus Juris* of the later empire was dogmatically taken as a perfect scheme of jurisprudence, and the innovations of the exegete were obscured and hidden, as it were, by his method of interpretation. The exegesis of the medieval Romanist was a purely logical dissection of the source with very little historical perspective, as in the method of scholasticism generally. And this had enabled him to reshape the meaning of the text by casuistic distinctions and analogies without denying its authority.

With the later Renaissance, however, the premise of medieval Romanism was indirectly undermined by new methods of interpretation. The academic jurists of the sixteenth century, and those of France especially, were deeply influenced by the humanist ideals of classical erudition and logical simplicity. Hence, instead of providing abstract interpretation, they now attempted to treat the *Corpus Juris* philologically, to restore the original meaning of the legal sources by relating them to all that was known about the ancient world. And instead of making casuistic distinctions and analogies, they attempted to expound the contents of the *Corpus Juris* as the logical components of a single system. Each of these reforms of method was originally intended by the humanists as an improvement of Romanistic jurisprudence and not as an attack upon its premises. But the more intensive their research in Roman history, and the more stringent their demand for system, the more the humanists were brought to the conclusion that the codification of Justinian was somewhat less than perfect or complete—that many of its rules were peculiar to the special needs of Rome, that much of Roman legal wisdom had been omitted or imperfectly recorded, and that what was actually included was often inconsistent or chaotic. The unintended direction of their enterprise, accordingly, was a break with the intellectual authority of Rome.

The final consummation of this break was the work of Jean Bodin, whose writings in the field of public law reflected a tendency in later humanism towards a reconstruction of juristic science on a base of universal history. In Bodin's system the principles of public law are no longer based, at least in theory, on an exposition of the law of Rome, or indeed of any other single system, but on a comparison and synthesis of all the juridical experience of all the most famous states. The uniformities of legal history, or the laws which "all or the greater part" of peoples have in common, are collected and synthetically expounded as the elements of public law which are essential to a social order.

The divergencies in history, conversely, or the laws peculiar to one state or another, are systematically classified in order to compare them and select the best. And finally these institutional diversities of peoples are correlated with major differences in their natural environment or political organization in order to discriminate the special factors which must be considered in evaluating laws. With Bodin, accordingly, a transition is finally effected from the exegesis of authority to a method of critical reflection and a general theory of law. And in some respects the natural law systems of the century which follows, as well as the comparative jurisprudence of the eighteenth century, are continuations of his program.

This juristic revolution, furthermore, was intimately related to the beginnings, in the sixteenth century, of a methodology or general theory of historical criticism. The program of Bodin and his associates was among the most intense expressions of the interest in universal history which is characteristic of the period in general. In the later Renaissance it was very seriously assumed that the reading of historians was the ideal form of political and moral education. And with this conviction the study of the past as such took on a status and importance which it had not known in classical antiquity. A complete familiarity with universal history was now regarded as a fundamental obligation of the educated man.

What was now required, therefore, was a method of historical instruction, or "art of reading" for the student, in the development of which the universal jurists played a leading role. To François Baudouin and Jean Bodin, a method for the study of the past was not only a general pedagogical objective, to which they were drawn by their interest in history, but a practical requirement of legal education, which was demanded by their views of jurisprudence. The methodological reflections of these jurists, therefore, are among the first significant attempts to explain all the principles of caution and to provide all the types of information which seemed of value in the reading of historians.

With this formulation of an art of reading, the writers of the sixteenth century were confronted with problems in the use of sources which up to now had never been considered systematically. Systematic reflection on the art of history, as it had been transmitted from the ancient world and continued by the early humanists, was primarily an "art of writing." And its essential problem was to construct the literary standards of an ideal narrative from evaluations of the classic models. In the "art of reading," on the other hand, all historians, of all varieties, were considered as a stock of sources for the study of the past. And from this perspective such questions inevitably arose as the logical basis of historical belief; the types of sources and their relative authority; the tests of documentary authenticity; and the indications of an author's biases. In one way or another, to be sure, certain aspects of these questions had been touched upon before. But it was only with the formulation of an art of reading that they were systematically related and developed as a methodology or theory of criticism.

Thus the third quarter of the sixteenth century was an important moment of transition in two areas of social thought. With the universal jurists of this period, and especially with Jean Bodin, a new foundation was established not only for jurisprudence and related social disciplines, but for the methodology of history as well. And since these transformations have not yet been adequately studied, the purpose of the present work is to explore their background and their outcome.

PART I

JURISPRUDENCE
FROM EXEGESIS OF THE ROMAN LAW
TO A COMPARATIVE METHOD

I

THE ROMAN LAW AND
MEDIEVAL JURISPRUDENCE

Scientific jurisprudence began in Europe around the end
of the eleventh century. With the urban revival, and the
growth of a more complicated social order generally, the
mechanisms of custom and tradition no longer sufficed
for the transmission and development of law. Professional
judges were required, as well as regular methods of instruction and formal techniques for the amplification of legal
rules. These growing needs could not be satisfied without
a systematic formulation of the basic principles and concepts of the legal order. But almost everywhere outside
of England the framework of juristic science was not
derived from reflection on domestic custom or even, in the
case of southern Europe, from those elements of written
law which had survived from Roman days. It was drawn
instead from the finished system of the Roman law as
represented by the compilation of Justinian. And from
the twelfth century to the sixteenth the characteristic form
of civil jurisprudence was the assimilation and adaptation
of the *Corpus Juris*.

The definite institution of this enterprise may be dated
from the formation of the law school of Bologna at the
end of the eleventh century.[1] At Bologna the materials of

[1] Paul Koschaker, *Europa und das römische Recht*, is perhaps the best
recent survey of the influence of Roman law in Europe. On the position

legal study encompassed the entire compilation of Justinian, and it was here, indeed, that the various components of the Roman law were gradually collated and ordered as a text which was to become the standard edition of the *Corpus Juris* up to the sixteenth century, and which is generally referred to as the medieval "vulgate." [2] At Bologna, furthermore, the study of the civil law became a fully independent discipline in no way subservient to the liberal arts of rhetoric and grammar.[3] The sources of the *Corpus Juris* were elaborately and repeatedly glossed from the technical standpoint of the jurist. And the text, thus clarified, was intensively expounded to the student in a systematic course of lectures.

The objectives of this program, as the glossators conceived it, was to make the Roman law available for legal practice, as though the codification of Justinian had never ceased to be in force.[4] Their grounds for this assumption can no longer be determined with complete assurance, and have been variously interpreted by scholars. The glossators may very well have felt that the *Imperium Romanum* of Justinian was directly continued in the Christian empire and that his legislation therefore was still valid.[5] But they

of Bologna in the early period see pp. 58–62, and see also Paul Vinogradoff, *Roman Law in Medieval Europe*, pp. 43–70.

2 It should be noted that in this edition of the *Corpus Juris* certain medieval sources were also included: a book of Lombard feudal customs, the *Libri Feudorum*, as well as several laws of German emperors. For the position of these in the "vulgate" see Friedrich Savigny, *Geschichte des römischen Rechts im Mittelalter*, III, ch. xxii.

3 Koschaker, *Europa und das römische Recht*, pp. 58, 69.

4 *Ibid.*, p. 67. See also Woldemar Engelmann, *Die Wiedergeburt der Rechtskultur in Italien*, p. 42.

5 Koschaker, *Europa und das römische Recht*, pp. 70, 79–80. This idea was not only deeply rooted in Italian consciousness but was vigorously promoted by the German emperors who would naturally benefit from a sense of continuity with Rome. Barbarossa, on one occasion, even spoke of "my predecessors Constantine, Valentinian, Justinian." See *ibid.*, p. 40, n. 3.

may also have looked upon the Roman Law as the common law of the Italian people; or they may have thought that the *Corpus Juris* was so obviously superior to any set of laws then known, that it had only to be explained to be accepted.[6] None of these motives is really in conflict with the others, and all may well have played a role. The result in any case, is clear. For one reason or another, the glossators of Bologna, like the later medieval jurists, looked upon the Roman Law as an immediately valid authority.[7]

But the most interesting point for our purposes is the close connection between this assumption of the glossators and their method of interpretation. Their idea that the *Corpus Juris* was immediately valid for their age went hand in hand with a lack of historical perspective. Like the medieval jurists who came after them, the lawyers of Bologna were generally unaware of any basic differences between their own society and the one for which their sources were intended; and they were even less aware of the social and intellectual differences among the various periods of Roman history which had contributed sources for Justinian's collection. In their interpretation of the text, accordingly, there was very little effort to explain the sense in terms of history. It was assumed, instead, that the *Corpus Juris*, by and large, was a self-contained and internally consistent whole, the rules of which were valid universally. And the method of interpretation was internal logical analysis.

This purely analytic standpoint is apparent from the nature of the glosses. Many of these, of course, are concerned with the proper reading of the text itself, and often cite variations between manuscripts. The great majority, however, are interpretations of a word or passage, the

---

[6] Engelmann, *Die Wiedergeburt der Rechtskultur in Italien*, p. 18.
[7] Koschaker, *Europa und das römische Recht*, p. 84.

sense of which was normally suggested to the glossator by his knowledge of related passages in other portions of the *Corpus*. Indeed, there are many glosses in which this process of internal comparison is made explicit, in the form of citations to related passages. And when one such passage is in apparent conflict with another, a distinction was sometimes offered to resolve the contradiction.[8] There are still other glosses which briefly comment on the rubric or title of a section of the *Corpus* in order to show how the legal contents included in the section are related to the leading concept.[9]

This analytic procedure was considerably more developed in the formal lectures of the glossators which were in the form of *summae titulorum*, or summations of the law according to the given subdivisions. In these expositions the reading of the text was preceded by an introductory survey of the contents of the title as a whole in order to explain the leading concepts. Each law or portion of the title was then presented with clarifications of its words and phrases. In the succeeding stage the implications of the contents were developed by adducing related "cases" from elsewhere in the *Corpus*. In the course of this, apparent contradictions were brought forward and resolved. And, finally, there was a deduction of *brocardica* or legal maxims implicit in the text and the solution of interesting questions.[10]

Thus the legal method of the glossators was broadly consonant with the scholastic form of science which was char-

[8] Engelmann, *Die Wiedergeburt der Rechtskultur in Italien*, p. 177; Savigny, *Geschichte des römischen Rechts im Mittelalter*, III, 532; Hermann Kantorowicz, *Studies in the Glossators of the Roman Law*, p. 33.
[9] Engelmann, *Die Wiedergeburt der Rechtskultur in Italien*, p. 177.
[10] Savigny, *Geschichte des römischen Rechts im Mittelalter*, III, 510–13; Enrico Besta, *L'Opera d'Irnerio*, I, 99–100. The form of these lectures was not, of course, invariable.

acteristic of the middle ages generally. The starting point
of science was a set of universal norms the truth of which
was taken on authority. And the essential task of thought
was to explicate the meaning of these elements by combination, distinction, and restatement. It is a well-known fact,
of course, that this scholastic method was not as servile as
its premises might indicate, for in the course of interpreting
authority the scholastic exegete could exercise considerable
freedom. And consciously or not, he could shape the meaning to his own experience and needs. Among the glossators, however, the technique of exegesis tended to be
relatively strict. Their major purpose was to make the
Roman Law available, to gain an elementary mastery over
the vast materials presented by their sources, and it was
therefore natural enough that they should adhere rather
closely to the text.

On the other hand, the commentators of the later middle ages asserted an ever greater freedom. One reason
for this change, perhaps, is that by the thirteenth century
the *Corpus Juris* had been glossed in its entirety and the
findings of the early school had been compiled and summarized in the *glossa ordinaria* of Accursius. The later
commentators, therefore, were no longer required to con-
centrate on elementary exegesis, but were free to consider
more speculative questions.[11] But the deeper cause, no
doubt, was the growing involvement of the medieval
Romanist with the problems of contemporary practice.[12]
By the thirteenth century the *Corpus Juris*, or at least
the portion of it covered by the gloss, had received widespread recognition as a common law. In most of Italy and
in southern Europe generally its prescription was enforced

---

[11] Engelmann, *Die Wiedergeburt der Rechtskultur in Italien*, p. 205.
[12] *Ibid.*, chs. II, III, and esp. pp. 204–42; Koschaker, *Europa und das
römische Recht*, ch. 8.

in court unless it was specifically in conflict with a custom or statute of the local jurisdiction. But with this penetration of the *Corpus Juris* into practice, the courts looked not only to the *glossa ordinaria* but also to contemporary commentators for authoritative guides to its interpretation. The doctors of the law schools were increasingly expected to provide solutions for contemporary issues. It may be noted further that this more immediate concern with practice was encouraged not only by judicial problems but also by political controversy, for the Roman Law was a basic source of arguments in jurisdictional disputes between the emperor and the pope, and between the Italian communes or territorial monarchies on the one hand and the pope or the emperor on the other.

Corresponding to these new responsibilities imposed upon the legists there was a shift in the technique of exegesis from literal to free interpretation. Since this freer form of exegesis was fully cultivated in Italy, it became known in other parts of Europe as the *mos docendi Italicus*, or Italian way of teaching, and it is also identified as "Bartolism" after Bartolus of Sassoferrato, its most celebrated master. This "Italian method," as it was known to Bodin and his contemporaries, may be conveniently illustrated by a mnemonic distich in which a writer of the sixteenth century summarized his technique of exposition.

In treating a title of the *Corpus*, says M. Gribaldus Mopha:

> Praemitto, scindo, summo, casumque figuro
> Perlego, do causas, connoto, objicio.[13]

According to this formula the "Italian" exegesis, which purported to be a comment on the text, did not even list

[13] From his *De methodo ac ratione studendi libri tres*, quoted in R. Stintzing, *Geschichte der deutschen Rechtswissenschaft*, I, 107. What follows is broadly based on Stintzing's account.

its contents until the stage of *perlegere*. Before "I read," in other words, there was a general discussion of the nature of the text and a free definition of its terms and concepts (*praemitto*); a breakdown of the various rules and principles involved and the formulation of maxims for further analysis (*scindo*); a general summation elaborated by references to leading commentators; and then a presentation of illustrative cases either from the *Corpus Juris* or the writer's own experience and imagination (*summo casumque figuro*). In none of these initial operations was the author bound to the terms, order, or even contents of the *Corpus Juris*. The introduction to the text was a purely dialectical and casuistic procedure—which meant that the original intention of the sources could be easily reshaped.

After the *perlegere*, or actual reading of the text, there was a further set of operations in which the main objective was the free development of implications. *Causas dare* meant an explanation of the rules according to the four Aristotelian causes, although this might sometimes be done in the *praemittere*. In the more important stage of *connotare*, there was an exploration of related passages—involving the resolution of apparent contradictions and the indication of interesting parallels as well as the extraction of general maxims—which became an extended legal commentary as opposed to the relatively modest notations of the glossators. *Objicere*—the final stage—meant to raise and to resolve objections. This, for the commentator, was the supreme test of legal virtuosity. The aim was to assemble every apparent contradiction to the author's opinion—from other commentators, from canon and customary law, from contemporary practice, and from the author's own imagination—and then to answer each objection by distinction, limitation, or amplification of received opinion. It is here indeed that we find a use of dialectic so subtle and refined as to make it seem that any opinion whatsoever could be wrung from traditional authority.

The Italian mode of exegesis was thus extremely free and, if one wills, "inaccurate." Yet this precisely was its strength. For it was the freedom of the *mos italicus* which enabled medieval jurists to reshape the *Corpus Juris* to the needs of medieval Europe while still maintaining its traditional authority. And it may perhaps be useful to illustrate this process from the work of Bartolus in the field of public law where the need for creative adaptation was particularly marked.[14]

For Bartolus, the civilian, the Roman Law was the law of the Roman Empire, and according to his law books the supreme power should properly belong to the German successors of Justinian. This same Bartolus, however, taught law in the city of Perugia and was a consultant to Italian cities which had claims to power of their own. Bad enough that even in the days of the glossators these cities had exercised executive and legislative rights inconsistent with imperial sovereignty as defined by Roman Law. Now that the empire was decaying even as a pretense they were asserting a *plentitudo potestatis*, and this was demanded not only by the Italian cities, which Bartolus mainly had in view, but by the kingdoms of the north as well, especially by France. How was it possible, then, to square the law books with reality?

Bartolus' answer was to "distinguish" the independent city as a special class among the *civitates* mentioned in the *Corpus Juris*. It is a *civitas* which does not acknowledge a

---

[14] The following account should not give the impression that Bartolus' views are systematic. They are, for the most part, widely scattered in his *Commentaries*. I should also add that the following remarks are not intended to show Bartolus' contributions to the theory of sovereignty, etc. At present I wish only to illustrate the potentialities of the exegetic method.

superior (*civitas superiorem non recognoscens*), and therefore a *civitas sibi princeps* which is a law unto itself.[15] But
in what sense can such a *civitas* still be considered a member of the empire? It continues to "hold" of the emperor
in some *de jure* sense, says Bartolus, because it has acquired
its rights by his consent—whether given overtly by concession or tacitly by long acquiescence of the emperor to
a known usurpation of his rights.[16] If this be so, then how
can the *civitas sibi princeps* be distinguished from a city
which still acknowledges the emperor as superior but
which enjoys the *merum* or pure *imperium*, described in
the *Corpus Juris* as the highest power?[17] And how can
the powers of either type of *civitas* be distinguished from
the powers of the emperor? The answer of Bartolus is to
subdivide the "pure *imperium*" according to its territorial
expanse and dignity. The power of the *civitas sibi princeps*
is limited to a single territory and does not bring the highest dignity. That of the ordinary city with *merum imperium* is lower still in dignity and may be limited in certain
functions (although Bartolus rarely specifies). That of the
emperor is highest in dignity because its scope is universal.

[15] Cecil N. S. Woolf, *Bartolus of Sassoferrato*, pp. 155–56.

[16] "You are aware that the *civitates* of Italy do not ordinarily have
the pure *imperium*, but have taken it by usurpation. I say, however, that
if a *civitas* wishes to justify itself and to exercise the pure and the mixed
imperium, it must allege a concession of the *Princeps*, or else a very
long period of time, in which the said *civitas* has exercised the pure
imperium in the case where it was not approved by a concession of the
Princeps. Yet if it prove that it has exercised the pure *imperium*, it is
valid." Latin quoted by Woolf, *ibid.*, pp. 135–36; translation mine. Prescription, it should be noted, is held possible only where power was
taken with the knowledge of the emperor, *patientia et scientia principis*.
Hence Bartolus doubts whether a valid usurpation can be accomplished
during an interregnum. *Ibid.*, p. 140.

[17] "There are certain *civitates*, which may recognize a superior, but
have the pure and the mixed *imperium* by the concession of the *Princeps*, and possess other *regalia* (such as those which are laid down in
Feudis, tit. *Quae sint regalia*)." Quoted by Woolf, *ibid.*, p. 138.

The emperor, however, has no power within the *civitates* because he is the master of the whole *qua* whole and not the ruler of its parts.[18] Within the empire as an all-inclusive *universitas*, therefore, there can be a variety of powers which, although independent, form a hierarchy. This leads to yet another question which, for the moment, we shall take as final. If there exists a plurality of legislative powers, how can one speak of a universal civil law? The solution, essentially, is that the *Corpus Juris* is binding as a "written reason," and not by legislative fiat. The legislative powers may adapt it to circumstances but they may not change its basic rules.

This analysis clearly depends on remarkable reinterpretations of the original meaning of the Roman concepts. The *civitas sibi princeps* is a "case" of *civitas* which violates the very notion of its class, for in later Roman public law subdivisions of the empire were invariably subordinate. The sovereignty of the emperor, which was monopolistic in the Roman system, is now interpreted as alienable and, bolder still, prescriptible. The empire itself, moreover, is regarded less as a system of political subordination than as a set of communities which recognize a single common law. And, conversely, the *Corpus Juris* which was originally enacted as a code by the power of a Roman emperor, is now presented as a kind of European common law which is not necessarily associated with political subordination to the emperor.

These distortions, however, are clearly something more than mere caprice. The solutions of Bartolus, like those

18 "I say that the emperor is truly lord of the entire world. And this does not prevent that others should be lords in a more particular sense, because the world is a kind of *universitas*, and hence there may be a person who possesses the said *universitas*, and yet the individual things do not belong to him." Quoted by Woolf, *ibid.*, p. 22, n. 4; translation mine.

of other lawyers of his time, were a reasonably close approximation to the pattern of territorial communities that was emerging in the later middle ages. They constitute in fact, if not explicitly, a creative adaptation of the Roman concepts to the legal needs of Europe. This work of adaptation, furthermore, is to be found in every area of jurisprudence, although not always in a fashion quite so striking. And it may be said in general, accordingly, that the actual function of the commentators with respect to Roman Law "was in no way purely passive, but legally creative in a high degree."[19]

But it is also apparent, on the other hand, that the creative achievement of medieval jurisprudence depended upon a pair of premises which it had never attempted to establish scientifically: the assumption, first, that the Roman Law is intrinsically perfect; and second, that the Roman Law as it was taught to medieval students was identical with the law of Rome as it was understood by Justinian. Neither of these premises, of course, could survive a critical appraisal. And both, as I shall now attempt to show, were fatally undermined by new methods of interpretation which developed in the sixteenth century.

[19] Koschaker, *Europa und das römische Recht*, p. 94.

II

THE HUMANIST REFORMS OF METHOD
AND THE BEGINNING
OF A CRITICAL PERSPECTIVE

The essence of this new approach was the application of humanist ideals of classical erudition and systematic presentation to the teaching of the Roman Law. Our purpose in what follows is not to trace the ramifications of this program in detail but only to illustrate its leading tendencies, and for this reason two simplifications will be made. Although the motifs of legal humanism were often developed in conjunction, we shall examine each component separately. And although the movement for reform was international in scope, with many local variations, we shall draw our illustrations mainly from the French whose contributions are generally regarded as the high point.

THE PHILOLOGISTS

For France, at least, the attack on medieval jurisprudence may be roughly dated from the publication, in 1508, of Guillaume Budé's *Annotationes in Pandectas*. Significantly enough, the author of this work wrote not as a lawyer but a humanist. Budé, indeed, had undergone some training in the law. But he was to be known primarily as a student of classical antiquities, a friend and ally of Erasmus, and the leading apostle of the Renaissance in France. And he undertook his study of the *Digest* as part of his vocation as a humanist.[1] The task, as the humanists conceived it, was to rejuvenate the arts and sciences by returning to the "classics" of antiquity,[2] which meant, in jurisprudence, a direct appreciation of the classic legal wisdom which had been excerpted and collected by Justinian. But these ancient sources, it was felt, could not appear in all their splendor until the errors and distortions of centuries of barbarism had first been cleansed away, and this precisely was the burden which Budé now undertook.[3] In his *Annotations to the Digest* he brings to bear a formidable mass of erudition and a highly sophisticated philological technique in order to determine the original reading of the text and the original usage of the terms and phrases.

Budé, it should be noted, was not the first to form this project. Attacks on the barbarous style of professional lawyers together with invitations to a renewed study of the classic sources had been an early theme among Italian humanists.[4] Such was the import, for example, of a famous preface by Laurenzo Valla which Budé refers to as a

---

[1] The best available account of Budé's life and work is Louis Delaruelle, *Guillaume Budé, les origines, les débuts, les idées maîtresses.* See esp. ch. III, pp. 93–129.

[2] For the nature of the humanist movement see Paul Oskar Kristeller, *Renaissance Thought*, pp. 1–23.

[3] ". . . Not only did I discover that the books themselves in many places were partly mutilated, partly erroneous, but (something which I thought much more disgraceful) I also noticed many words, not of common but of good and ancient coinage, which had been translated into an alien usage owing to the ignorance of the times. Moved by indignation I dared, now long ago, to boast too rashly and boldly to my friends that I would see to it one day that the *Digest* would be read more correctly and intelligently." *Annotationes Gulielmi Budaei in quatuor et viginti Pandectarum libros*, p. 17.

[4] For a concise history of juridical humanism in this period see Domenico Maffei, *Gli inizi dell'umanesimo giuridico.* The polemics of the humanists are treated in Part I.

source of inspiration.[5] Towards the end of the fifteenth century, moreover, Angelo Poliziano had begun to compare the text of the medieval vulgate with the oldest extant version of the *Digest*, the *Littera Florentina* or *Codex Pisanus*, which was normally kept from the scrutiny of scholars, and he had already noted significant discrepancies —above all in the rendering of terms in Greek—which had led him to contemplate a critical edition.[6] But this and similar work, of which Budé was cognizant,[7] was but the preface to a philological critique. Budé it was who first attempted extended, detailed annotation.

The result, inevitably, was to portray a large part of medieval jurisprudence as a misinterpretation of the ancient Roman Law, and thus to discredit the scholastic method. Budé, to begin with, detected innumerable instances in which the medieval edition of the *Corpus Juris* seemed to have been based upon defective manuscripts, or corrupted by the errors of copyists, and therefore in conflict with the probable text of the original. These errors, furthermore, were often crucial to the sense. Some sixty years later François Hotman, summarizing the work of Budé and his successors, scornfully noted that the medieval vulgate was often grossly and nonsensically corrupt. Passages with negative force in the original often appeared in the vulgate as affirmative, and vice versa. The gender of terms was frequently inverted. And in many places the reference was inside out, as when things pertaining to the plaintiff were assigned to the defendant, or things con-

---

[5] *Annotationes . . . in quatuor et viginti Pandectarum libros*, p. 16. The preface in question is to Book III of Valla's *De linguae latinae elegentia libri sex.*

[6] Maffei, *Gli inizi dell'umanesimo giuridico*, pp. 88 ff., Stintzing, *Geschichte der deutschen Rechtswissenschaft*, I, 175 ff. For a general survey of the scholarly activities of Italian juridical humanists prior to Budé see Maffei, Part II, chs. I–III.

[7] Delaruelle, *Guillaume Budé*, p. 103.

cerning heirs to legatees. In Hotman's view, at least, the list of errors could be expanded indefinitely.[8]

Budé discovered, furthermore, that even where the text was accurate the sense had frequently been misinterpreted through ignorance of classical culture. In many difficult cases the *glossa ordinaria* gave no interpretation whatsoever, presumably because the terms seemed impenetrably alien; in other cases its suggestions were partial or misleading; and in many others its renderings were flatly incorrect. A simple but clear example of these last is the gloss of Accursius on a passage in *Dig.* I, 16 (Tit. *De officio proconsulis, l. proconsules*). The passage reads: *Proconsules non amplius quam sex fascibus utuntur*, which means, as Budé shows, that proconsuls are entitled to no more than six *fasces*. Accursius, however, interprets *fascibus* (the bundles of rods carried before a magistrate by lictors) to mean "months." Hence the meaning to Accursius is that the term of a proconsul in his office is more than six months, and he feels confirmed in this opinion by a passage in *Dig,* I, 2 (Tit. *De origine juris*) which refers to a term of six months in connection with the dictator.[9] Misinterpretations of this sort can lead very easily, of course, to apparent contradictions between one law and another, or within a single law. And it thus turns out, according to Budé, that the celebrated "antinomies" discovered by the medieval jurists were often the result of simple ignorance, and that the ingenious solutions which were offered were not only so much labor wasted but often compoundings of initial errors.[10]

[8] François Hotman, *Antitribonianus sive dissertatio de studio legum*, in *Variorum opuscula ad cultiorem jurisprudentiam adsequendam pertinentia*, VII, 205–6.

[9] *Annotationes Gulielmi Budaei in quatuor et viginti Pandectarum libros*, p. 166.

[10] See, for example, *Annotationes reliquae in Pandectas*, p. 28, annotation *iusta uxor*.

Yet another charge against the medieval jurist was his ignorance of Roman legal history. In interpreting a legal institution, Budé frequently attempts to show its variations in the course of time. For example, in his discussion of the Roman treasury he finds important variations between the periods before and after Constantine.[11] His most remarkable achievements, however, are probably to be found in an extensive comment, amounting almost to a monograph, on the constitution of the Roman senate.[12] One result of such historical dissections is to show that the contents of the *Digest*, having been assembled from different periods of Roman history, were not always completely homogeneous and frequently could not be understood by logical analysis alone. Here again the analytic method of the medieval jurist was a fertile source of misconceptions. Accursius, Budé remarks, "took note of neither histories nor annals; and such questions as when did jurisconsults, legislators, or emperors live, or who among these were contemporaries, were of no concern to him. But if this be so (as certainly it is) how could this man have been sure of his opinion in view of the great variations in the law from one century to another? Many antinomies, indeed, cannot be resolved or explained without an understanding of this fact, of which Accursius was ignorant. And what is surely to be reckoned even more pernicious is the fact that he has generally induced his followers (who comprise the majority of legists) to swear unhesitatingly (as I might say) upon these very errors." [13]

There are, finally, two further tendencies in Budé's work which point beyond the errors of the medieval jurist to defects of the Roman Law itself. His philological approach inevitably focused on the relationship of Roman Law to

11 *Annotationes . . . in quatuor et viginti Pandectarum libros,* p. 150.
12 *Ibid.,* pp. 96 ff.   13 *Ibid.,* p. 42.

the specific circumstances under which it was produced. It is, in fact, the peculiarities of Roman institutions on which Budé lays the greatest emphasis. And he frequently attempts to clarify a Roman practice by contrasting it with European counterparts, as in his treatment of the Roman Senate. The result, accordingly, is to suggest that much of Roman Law was historically particular, and thus to undermine the notion that it was the very measure of a universal law.

Moreover, Budé the scholar and the humanist was not only ready but extremely eager to affirm his own understanding of the sources against that of Justinian's commissioners. He is no longer willing, on Justinian's authority, to exclude the existence of "antinomies" within the *Corpus Juris*, and to assume, as had Accursius, that "no two statements in the law are *contraria* or *similia*." [14] In Budé's opinion at least some of the antinomies discovered in the *Corpus Juris* were real and not apparent contradictions which could only be explained by the occasional failure of Justinian's jurists to detect and fully to eliminate conflicts of doctrine among the different sources of their compilation. In one section of the *Annotationes* a list of such antinomies is offered in order to support the finding "that there seem to be several different places in the *Digest* where Tribonian is caught napping in bringing things together." [15] The wider implications of this criticism are not as yet explored. But the general tendency of Budé's whole perspective is to undercut the traditional assumption that the *Corpus Juris* is a perfectly consistent system.

On every level, therefore, the *Annotationes* of Budé involves a major break with the premises and method of the *mos Italicus*. And it may be noted briefly that it is not in any sense an isolated effort but helped to launch a

[14] *Ibid.*, p. 351.   [15] *Ibid.*, p. 351.

powerful trend in contemporary jurisprudence. In its
polemical aspect, Budé's work is one of the important
sources for that contemptuous image of the medieval jurist
which became extremely widespread in the sixteenth century and is sometimes encountered even now. Budé himself, on some occasions, was willing to concede that Bartolus and Accursius were men of earnestness and talent
who were hampered in the search for truth by the "ignorance" in which their age was sunk. But against those whom
Budé calls "Accursiani," those recent and contemporary
jurists who "slavishly" adhere to traditional authorities, his
invective is immoderately bitter. These are "rather stupid
men who are willing to believe, with closed eyes, that their
authorities, who had no true Latinity, were able, nonetheless, to give the very best interpretation of the highly Latin
writings of the *Digest*." [16] To this and other comments in
Budé the parallel in Rabelais is obvious, for the Rabelaisian
caricature of the pompous windbag, speaking pidgin Latin,
responding to every question with an inane mumbo jumbo
of irrelevant citations, bordering the pure pages of the
Corpus Juris with a crusted excrement of glosses,[17] and

[16] *Ibid.*, p. 141.

[17] Says Pantagruel in the second book, ch. X: "Ay, you have buried
the issue under the dung of a thousand old mastiffs who have never
grasped the simplest law of the *Pandects,* of blockheads and tithe-calves,
of dolts lacking the rudiments that make it possible to begin to understand the law. Did they know Greek and Latin? Certainly not. Well,
what did they know? Merely the Gothic and Barbarian tongues. Yet
Ulpian tells us in his *Liber de Origine Juris, of the Origin of Law,* that
our code came from the Greeks. Isn't it full of Greek words and sentences? From the Greek, then, it was translated into Latin, into the
purest, most admirable style conceivable in that language. And, as I say
this, I do not forget Sallust, Varro, Cicero, Seneca, Livy or Quintilian.
How then could these old dullards appreciate the text of the laws when
they never clapped eyes on a decent Latin book? Their style suffices to
prove it: it is the style of chimney sweeps, cooks, and scullions, not
jurists.

"Besides, the law grew up out of the field of moral and natural philoso-

finally settling the interminable cases of his hapless litigants by throwing dice,[18] differs from Budé's descriptions only in its coarseness. In Rabelais, therefore, we have something more than the image of the people. Similar indictments of the *mos Italicus* formed the standard preface to almost every great work of French jurisprudence in the sixteenth century. By Bodin's time they had become something of a routine formula.[19]

On its positive side, and more importantly, Budé's pro-

phy. Then how could these idiots construe it when by God they studied less philosophy than the average mule? The humanities, a knowledge of antiquity, history? In these subjects your dotards were about as well equipped as a toad is with feathers. Yet, without these, the law is unintelligible, as I intend to prove more fully in a future work."

"Very well, then: if you want me to handle this suit, first burn up all this trash. Then summon the two parties before me. When I have heard them, I shall give you my opinion without pretence or reservation." *The Five Books of Gargantua and Pantagruel*, trans. Jacques le Clercq (New York, 1936), pp. 203–4.

[18] The reference is to Rabelais' story of Judge Bridlegoose, who settles cases by a throw of dice. *Ibid.*, Bk. III, chs. XXIX–XLIII, pp. 438–56. This does not mean, however, that the judge is in any way contemptuous of legal forms. On the contrary, the throw of dice is only the logical culmination of an elaborate procedure all of which is defended by the judge through learned exegesis of the medieval sources. Indeed, the throw of dice itself is governed by most refined prescriptions. For example, in doubtful cases the use of small dice is demanded according to the well-known maxim, *Semper in obscuris quod minimum est sequimur*, literally, "In obscure situations we follow what is least" (p. 441). The judge, it is pointed out, had been applying such methods for some forty years on the bench during which time every one of his decisions had been ratified by the superior court (p. 430).

[19] The inevitable image is the contrast between the wilderness of medieval jurisprudence and the gardens of humanist instruction. And so Bodin: "It should cause no wonder, therefore, if youth was greatly discouraged in the past when it was summoned from the sweetest flowers of the disciplines, from the charming gardens of philosophy and eloquence, to the rough and jagged rocks, and the brush and brambles of the old interpreters." Jean Bodin, *Oratio de instituenda in republica juventute ad senatum populumque tolosatem* (1559), in *Oeuvres philosophiques de Jean Bodin*, ed. Pierre Mesnard, Vol. V, 3 of the *Corpus général des philosophes français*, 17B. The same image is used in the preface to Bodin's *Methodus*.

gram of research was taken over and developed by a new school of academic jurists who sought to teach directly from the sources, to the more or less complete exclusion of the gloss and commentaries. But the sources, as Budé and others had insisted, were first to be restored and purified before they could be profitably studied. And hence the teaching program of these jurists went hand in hand with vast researches in Roman legal history, the fruits of which are among the most impressive monuments of Renaissance scholarship. It may be noted, furthermore, that cultivated scholarship, and juridical humanism generally, became closely identified with France and were known in Europe as the *mos docendi Gallicus*. The early leaders, to be sure, had included the Italian jurist, Andrea Alciato, and the German, Ulrich Zasius, who constituted, with Budé, the threesome saluted by Erasmus as the *triumviratus constituendae rei pandectariae*.[20] But the French universities were relatively more receptive to the new approach than those of other parts of Europe. And it was in France, therefore, and at the school of Bourges especially, that juridical humanism was to find its most numerous and most brilliant exponents—among whom Jacques Cujas was perhaps preeminent.[21]

We may anticipate, however, that this spread of a philo-

---

[20] Coleman Phillipson, "Andrea Alciati and his Predecessors," in *Great Jurists of the World*, Continental Legal History Series, II, 71.

[21] Koschaker, *Europa und das römische Recht*, p. 109. See also Maffei, *Gli inizi dell'umanesimo giuridico*, pp. 162 ff. and Stintzing, *Geschichte der deutschen Rechtswissenschaft*, I, 122 ff. For a brief but fairly complete catalogue of the "cultivated school" in the sixteenth century, see L. Palazzini Finetti, *Storia della ricerca delle interpolazioni nel Corpus Juris Giustineaneo*, ch. IV.

The question as to the causes of this French preeminence is not considered here because a satisfactory answer would depend upon exhaustive research into the precise relationship of academic jurisprudence and legal practice in different parts of Europe. For general reference to this issue, see Koschaker, pp. 123–24, and D. Maffei as cited above.

logical approach to Roman Law would encourage attacks
on its intellectual authority. The more they worked upon
the sources the more convinced the humanists became that
much of Roman Law was peculiar to its time and place and
that the *Corpus Juris* was neither the entirety of Roman
legal wisdom nor even a consistent whole. These conclusions, to be sure, were quite compatible with continuing respect for Roman law and willingness to borrow from its
sources. But in principle at least it was increasingly difficult
to look upon the *Corpus Juris* as the very model of a reasonable law, valid for every time or place. What was now
demanded, therefore, was the reconstruction of juristic science on a more truly universal basis. And there was, as
we shall now attempt to show, yet another motive for this
break in the various efforts of the humanists to make a
"system" of the law.

THE SYSTEMATISTS

In the middle of the sixteenth century the program of
juristic humanism had come to include not only a philological preparation of the sources but a more or less extensive rearrangement in order to achieve greater clarity and
ease of comprehension. The immediate impetus was the
painful gap between the length and complexity of legal
education and the ideal of "art" or "system" promoted by
humanist principles of rhetoric and logic. In his teaching
of the *Corpus Juris* the medieval lawyer was not particularly concerned to show how each component was related
to the logic of the whole. The individual topic was considered, for the most part, from a purely casuistic standpoint. It was related to the sources as a whole only in so
far as passages from elsewhere in the *Corpus* were brought
to bear on the analysis from one perspective or another,
and introduced *ad hoc* in order to develop implications

and distinctions. Hence, like any exegetic method, the *mos Italicus* tended to fragment the system of the text.[22] And the structure of the whole was all the more obscured by the custom of elaborate digressions to comment on the opinions of previous commentators. In the *mos Italicus*, accordingly, assimilation of the *Corpus Juris* heavily depended on the sheer ability to assimilate a mass of unrelated details, which was one of the reasons why it required from five to seven years to complete a course of study in the Roman Law.[23]

Against all this, however, there now appeared a humanist ideal of teaching which rejected casuistic exegesis in favor of "methodical" or systematic exposition. This new objective, which was deeply influenced by rhetoric, and developed by logicians of the age as the principle of "art" or "method," was the articulation of a body of knowledge around a single scheme of concepts, moving in order from the most general down to the most particular by some consistent principle of classification or division.[24] And since the

---

[22] "But whether it be mere incomprehension or legally creative instinct which guides the exegetes, the influence of both was only made possible in this degree through the predominance of analysis, the result of which is to separate the individual elements from the intellectual context which conditions them and to consider them as independent entities. Thus isolated, the individual passage, interpreted through arguments which seem conclusive for the given case, can be given a meaning against which it is protected as soon as it is considered as an organic member of a whole, as the consequence of a higher legal concept. But precisely this synthetic mode of treatment was reduced to the barest minimum through distinction and casuistry.

"As long as the traditional method remains in full force, the dissolution of knowledge into an unsurveyable mass of individual elements seems not to be a lack of art but rather an unavoidable difficulty inherent in the nature of the positive law, and one which must be overcome by strength of memory in a course of study lasting many years." Stintzing, *Geschichte der deutschen Rechtswissenschaft*, I, 113–14.

[23] For a review of contemporary complaints, see *ibid.*, pp. 129–32.

[24] A highly influential example of a "method" in this sense is Peter Ramus' idea of a "collocation" of arguments or a "distribution" of a

given structure of the *Corpus Juris*, whatever else its virtues, was surely deficient by this test, the humanist lawyers of the sixteenth century embarked on ever more elaborate and far-reaching rearrangements, the aim of which was *jus in artem redigere*—the reduction of the law to system.[25] In the earlier phase the efforts of the systematists, among whom the most influential, once again, were French, centered mainly on rearranging the fragments of the compilation, while the basic subdivisions, as represented by the titles, were accepted more or less as given.[26] Such, for example, was the general position of François Duaren (Duarenus) in his influential letter to Gaillart on the reform of legal education (1544).[27] Later on, however, with the

concept among its parts. "The second phase [of judgment] . . . provides a *Collocation*, an order of many and various arguments coherently related to each other, as though an unbroken chain of links, and related to a single certain goal. Of this disposition the two principal parts are *definition* and *distribution*. For the thing must first be defined and explained as a whole, and next divided into parts . . ." (*Dialecticae institutiones* [original edition, 1543] in Antonius Goveanus, *Opera*, p. 734. For the influence of Ramus' and similar ideas of method of jurisprudence see Stintzing, *Geschichte der deutschen Rechtswissenschaft*, I, 145–50. The influence of Ramus on Bodin is very nicely worked out in Kenneth D. McRae, "Ramist Tendencies in the Work of Jean Bodin," *Journal of the History of Ideas*, XVI, 306–23. For a discussion of ideas of method in this period see Neal W. Gilbert, *Renaissance Concepts of Method*.

[25] The origin of this slogan is a lost work by Cicero, *De jure civili in artem redigendo*, mentioned in Aulus Gellius, *Noctes atticae*, I, 22. Cicero also uses the phrase and mentions the problem in *De oratore*, I, 41. Among the reasons, says Cicero, why the study of the law remains so difficult is that "there have been none who have arranged its contents in an artful manner according to their main divisions. For nothing can be reduced to art (*ad artem redigi possit*) unless the person who has mastered those things of which he wishes to institute the system is in possession of that science by which an art can be made of those things of which as yet there is no art." It may also be noted that demands for an *ars juris* in this sense were an early theme among the humanists. See, for example, Budé, *Annotationes . . . in quatuor et viginti Pandectarum libros*, p. 8.

[26] Stintzing, *Geschichte der deutschen Rechtswissenschaft*, I, 142 ff.

[27] *Ibid.*, p. 371.

constant deepening of critical awareness, the even more radical project was conceived of reworking the entire system. François Connan, the first to try it, was prevented by an untimely death. But towards the end of the century a total system of the civil law, the result of thirty years of labor on the sources, was published by Hugues Doneau (Donellus).[28] And it is his work which is generally regarded as the high point of the systematic movement.[29]

The ultimate effect of all this work, however, was to add one more dimension to the "anti-Romanist" tendencies already latent in the work of the philologists. The systematic movement still assumed, of course, that the contents of the *Corpus Juris* were the pieces of a perfect system which had only to be "put in order." But it was now deliberately argued for the first time in the history of European jurisprudence that the established system was inadequate; and the more ambitious the attempts at rearrangement, the more indubitable it seemed that the *ratio scripta* of the middle ages had been composed by men who were deficient in juristic science.[30]

[28] The first volume appeared in 1589, in Germany, where Doneau was teaching as a Protestant refugee from France. Publication was completed only after his death in 1591. Stintzing, *Geschichte der deutschen Rechtswissenschaft*, I, 378.

[29] Thus Phillipson, "Jacques Cujas," *Great Jurists of the World*, II, 103, and also Stintzing, *Geschichte der deutschen Rechtswissenschaft*, I, 381, who speaks of *die beiden Heroen Cujas und Donell*. For German contributions to systematic reconstruction of the *Corpus Juris* see *ibid.*, pp. 241 ff. and 424 ff.

[30] It is not our purpose here to assess the justice of this criticism, but only to describe the emergence of a critical attitude. It should be pointed out, however, that the critical reaction of the sixteenth century is often overstated. The *Corpus Juris*, to be sure, is often unsystematic. See Koschaker, *Europa und das römische Recht*, pp. 63 ff. and esp. p. 65, and also H. F. Jolowicz, *Historical Introduction to the Study of Roman Law*, p. 493. But the systematists of the sixteenth century tend to overstate its defects—in part because they often do not fully understand its structure, and in part also because their humanist enthusiasm for the Republican age of Roman history tends to prejudice them against the

Thus, as the very title indicates,[31] the first chapter of Doneau's *Commentarii de jure civili* is a demonstration that the systematic principles intended by the authors of the *Corpus* have not been executed in the body of their work. The *Institutes* divide the realm of law into that which pertains to persons, things, and actions. As Doneau understands it, this involves a primary division of the law into a part which teaches us to recognize our rights, and a part which tells us how they are to be secured. The second part is the realm of legal actions. The first is divided into those rights which are inherent in the status of our person and those which arise from our relationship to things.[32] This scheme, however, is not reflected in the order of the sources. After a few remarks on the status of persons and the classes of things the *Digest* jumps directly to the forms of action. "Therefore, the authors inform us of the means of obtaining judgment of our rights before they have taught us what the rights may be which we can bring for judgment." [33]

Not only is there an inverted order of divisions, but no one division is carried through completely and consistently. For example, personal status, as a general idea, is nowhere explicitly defined. Although one might expect that its modes would be listed and explained in Part I of the *Digest* in titles devoted to the status of persons, important

---

legal culture of the later period. Warnings against humanist exaggerations may be found in Fritz Schultz, *History of Roman Legal Science*, pp. 265, 283, 321–22.

[31] "On the composition and arrangement of the Digest; what the author finds lacking in it which explains why he will not use it in these books." *Commentarii de jure civili*, in *Opera omnia*, I, 1.

[32] "The civil law . . . consists in these two things, or parts, and in this order:—in the recognition of what belongs to each, and in the means of obtaining what is recognized. . . ." "The right of each of us is placed partly in the person of each, and partly in external things. . . ." *Ibid.*, p. 3.

[33] *Ibid.*, p. 3.

forms of status are not developed at this place. The law of slavery, as well as the status of freedmen and the rights of patrons, is not taken up until Part VI. Under the status of persons, to be sure, the family is properly considered, but only in certain of its aspects, for one must look elsewhere for a full description of the father's power. One might also expect a consideration of tutelages at this point. "But where are these treated in the *Digest?* Only in the fourth part, at the end of a treatment of marriage—on the grounds, I suppose, that children come from marriages . . . as though anyone might be in tutelage or guardianship because he had the status of a son, and not because he was under age" [34] or otherwise incompetent. It seems to Doneau therefore that the rules of personal status are "often so severed from their head and cast so far away, that the last thing you would recognize to look at them is the body of which they are the limbs." [35]

A similar pattern seems to hold for things. There is no discussion of the subject generally. Titles dealing with public and sacred property are not subjoined to the title *De rerum divisione* (I, 8) but appear in widely scattered places. Thus *Ne quid in loco sacro* and *De mortuo inferendo*, both dealing with the law of sacred places, are found in Part VI (XLIII, 6) and Part II (XI, 8) respectively; and *Ne quid in loco publico*, which deals with public property, in Part VI (XLIII, 8). But even the relationships arising out of private things are not comprehended as a whole. Servitudes, obligations, acquisitions—and similar subdivisions of this concept—are literally scattered through the *Digest* in different parts and titles, *max-*

[34] *Ibid.*, p. 4. Note that a "part" of the *Digest* includes several books. Part IV includes Books XX–XXVII and the discussion of guardianship begins at Book XXVI.
[35] *Ibid.*, p. 3.

ime disjunctis locis. And even these lower subdivisions are never treated systematically. The law of things, therefore seems as disordered as the law of persons.[36] And what applies to things and persons is also true of actions.[37]

Equally serious is the disordered condition of the single titles. Their legal formulations are not the product of a single mind. They are composed of excerpts from the ancient writers, which are so diverse in provenance, so cryptic, and so fragmentary that their original meaning is frequently uncertain. These fragments, moreover, "may be better said to have been thrown or stuffed into the titles than collated." [38] They are introduced pell mell without regard to logic; fragments promised by the title are omitted; irrelevant excerpts are included; essential pieces turn up in other, widely separated places. The result of this disorder is confusion and uncertainty of meaning. The individual parts, severed from their original connections, derive no clear meaning from their present context. Conversely, "the meaning of the whole must inevitably be misconstrued where its parts cannot be understood or even recognized." [39]

It is Doneau's opinion that the *Corpus Juris* is disorderly on every level.[40] Reconstruction seems essential, therefore, not only for convenient presentation, but to determine the meaning of the contents. And if Justinian's authority be interposed as an objection to this enterprise, Doneau will not flinch from setting it aside. The power of emperors, he argues, extends no more to the science than to the language of the law. "From princes comes the law's authority; from learned men and skilled, the method and right order of its teaching." [41]

[36] *Ibid.,* pp. 4–5.   [37] *Ibid.,* p. 8.   [38] *Ibid.,* p. 9.   [39] *Ibid.*
[40] "Indeed, is there anything here which is rendered in its proper order?" *Ibid.,* Preface, p. xii.
[41] *Ibid.,* pp. 10–11.

For Doneau, to be sure, this criticism and this repudiation of authority extend only to the form of Roman Law. The contents, he assumes—in accordance with received tradition—will fall into a perfect, universal system once the key to their arrangement has been found.[42] And the key itself is given in the logic of the *Institutes*. This, he tells us, is the very premise of his work. He has added nothing to the sources but has retained and explicated everything.[43] So faithful to the contents are his commentaries that the most traditional of jurists can confidently use them as a guide through the labyrinth of Justinian. His critics, therefore, misread his true intentions. If he has changed the order of the law, it has been to save its contents, not to destroy them. The obscurities of the present compilation have already engendered an ignorant body of opinion which would repudiate the *Corpus* totally. Doneau's explication of its latent logic will elucidate the splendor of the system and disarm this sect of anti-Romanists.[44]

Nevertheless, the systematic school, however much it

[42] "Of the dignity and excellence of *Digest* and the *Code* it is impossible to say enough." "And indeed this law has been so well received by almost every people, and in almost every age from Justinian's time up to the present, that it is used by all the peoples in whatever matters the laws of a country are no obstacle." *Ibid.*, Preface, p. xi.

[43] "What, therefore, do we find lacking in this composition? If this is asked about the contents, nothing; and not only this, but these are the very selfsame contents which we use, and we bow to the composer in retaining and explaining them. But if of the order and arrangement: we look in vain for everything." *Ibid.*, p. 2.

[44] " 'What, then?' it may be asked by someone. 'Will you repudiate the civil law composed by Justinian, or rather by Julian, the most excellent of Jurisconsults?' The truth, indeed, is that I do not at all repudiate the civil law composed by the order of Justinian. On the contrary, I strive with all my might for its retention, for I am trying to explain it through my work, and as it were to bring it more and more into the light, so that it may even find approval among those who, failing to understand its force, reject it, in part as something unneeded in a commonwealth, and in part, even, as a pernicious thing by which litigations are fomented." *Ibid.*, pp. 9–10.

wished to "save" the Roman Law, dealt a cruel blow to
its authority. Doneau convicts Justinian and his jurists of
incompetence in legal science, and from their authority he
appeals to universal reason. He still assumes that the Roman
sources and universal reason come together in the *Corpus
Juris*, but only on the deepest level and after total rearrangement. Moreover, since the systematists were unable
to agree on the principles of rearrangement their essential
premise could easily be doubted. Doneau's interpretation
of the basic scheme significantly differed from Duaren's,
and Duaren's, again, from Connan's.[45] And it might therefore seem to follow that no system existed to be found, and
that the Roman Law was but a congeries of fragments.
For if—as Doneau seeks to demonstrate—the composers of
the *Corpus Juris* were ignorant of legal science, must one
automatically assume that the given fragments were reduc-
ible to system? Justinian, perhaps, had left out certain
necessary parts. The "epigones" of Roman jurisprudence
may have failed to select the best from their tradition. One
might even speculate that the legal wisdom of the Roman
people was something less than perfect in its content.
These, in fact, were the conclusions of the anti-Romanists.
But it was the systematists, ironically enough, who had
taken the critical initiative.

[45] On these divergencies see M. A. P. Th. Eyssell, *Doneau, sa vie et
ses ouvrages,* pp. 228–45.

III

THE ATTACK ON THE AUTHORITY
OF ROMAN LAW

Demands for the reorganization of jurisprudence on an independent and more universal basis began, in France, around the third quarter of the sixteenth century. The leading figures in this movement were Jean Bodin, François Hotman, and François Baudouin—each of whom, and especially the latter two, were leading exponents of the *mos docendi Gallicus*. The philological researches of Hotman and Baudouin were among the major contributions of the period to the history of Roman institutions. Hotman, moreover, had edited the works of Connan, and his *Partitiones juris civilis elementariae* (Basel, 1560) and Baudouin's *Juris civilis catechesis* (Basel, 1557), as well as Bodin's *Juris universi distributio*, in certain of its aspects, were systematic exercises in the Connanite tradition.[1] But by the 1560s all three writers had come to the conclusion that a systematic jurisprudence could not be erected on a purely Roman basis. And their proposals for a new foundation were now set down in very close succession. Baudouin's *De institutione historiae universae et ejus cum jurisprudentia conjunctione prolegomenon* was published in 1561. Hotman's *Antitribonianus* was composed in 1567,[2] and

---

[1] For the identification of these works as Connanite see *Oeuvres philosophiques de Jean Bodin*, ed. Mesnard, pp. 69–70.

[2] Although 1567 is usually taken as the date of publication, it is probable that the *Antitribonianus* was first published in 1603, thirteen years

Bodin's *Methodus ad facilem historiarum cognitionem* appeared in 1566. Hence, although the relationship of these three writers has not been fully clarified,[3] they may undoubtedly be grouped as "universalists."

In all three writers the theoretical grounds for an attack on Roman Law were derived from the critical work of the philologists and systematists. But an even broader background may be briefly noted in the growing respect, among jurists of this period, for the value of the customary law. The Roman Law had never been fully accepted by the French as an immediately binding common law. As *ratio scripta*, or the "reasonable law," its intellectual authority had always been considerable. And since local customs were often contradictory, defective, or obscure, it had been able, in the higher middle ages, to make significant inroads into practice, even in the "region of the customary law." But in the middle of the fifteenth century an exhaustive editing of the customs was begun, the ultimate effect of which was to slow the process of reception, and to prevent the Roman Law from achieving the status of a common law for France.[4] By a royal edict of 1454 the customs of each different region were to be officially collected, recorded, and confirmed. And by the sixteenth

---

after Hotman's death. J. van Kan, *Les efforts de codification en France*, p. 42, n. 1.

[3] The first discussion of Baudouin, Hotman, and Bodin as an ensemble is E. Fournol, "Sur quelques traités de droit public au XVIe siècle," *Nouvelle revue historique de droit français et étranger*, XXI, 298–325. Fournol notes that all three writers had a special interest in public law, that they found the *Corpus Juris* unrewarding in this field, and that they turned to history for new materials. He fails, however, to identify their general attack on the authority of Roman Law and its relation to the *mos docendi Gallicus*. The background for Bodin, however, is more adequately supplied in the more recent work of Jean Moreau-Reibel, *Jean Bodin et le droit publique comparé dans ses rapports avec la philosophie de l'histoire*, and John L. Brown, *The Methodus ad Facilem Historiarum Cognitionem of Jean Bodin: a Critical Study*.

[4] See J. Declareuil, *Histoire générale du droit français*, pp. 831–32.

century this work was already well advanced.[5] In this compilation of the customs, to be sure, there was a further borrowing of Roman concepts to correct or amplify the customs and to provide a systematic framework. But the ultimate result was to create a set of customary laws which, however Romanized in content, were now established in a written form. The jurists of the time, accordingly, subjected them to the kind of learned commentary which had been hitherto applied to Roman Law exclusively, and sought to understand and rationalize their contents.[6] And among those reformers who looked forward to unification of the laws of France, the common content of the customs was often taken as the basic starting point.[7] It was thus the hope of Du Moulin, the most celebrated student of the customary laws,[8] that a common code could be created by a critical comparison and synthesis of customs.[9]

But for the theory of jurisprudence the most important

[5] "La plupart des coutumes des pays coutumiers furent rédigées sous Louis XII, surtout de 1506 à 1510. . . . Beaucoup le furent encore sous François Ier . . . quelques-unes, mais plus rares, dans la seconde moitié du XVIe siècle. . . . Le travail se poursuivit même encore aux XVIIe et XVIIIe siècles, mais par des actes isolés et exceptionnels." A. Esmein, *Cours élémentaire d'histoire du droit français*, pp. 713–14. It is precisely in the 1550s that this work begins to be revised in a more scientific fashion as the result of practical experience and theoretical criticism. See *ibid.*, pp. 717 ff.

[6] Declareuil, *Histoire générale du droit français*, pp. 882–83.

[7] *Ibid.*, p. 882; Van Kan, *Les efforts de codification en France*, pp. 36–37.

[8] Esmein, *Cours élémentaire*, pp. 719–20, holds that of all his contemporaries Du Moulin had the greatest influence on legal practice.

[9] Charles Du Moulin (Molinaeus), *De concordia et unione consuetudinum franciae*, in *Tractatus commerciorum et usarum*. "Indeed," says Du Moulin, "there is nothing more useful and desirable for the entire commonwealth than the reduction of the highly diffuse and often most ineptly varying customs of this kingdom to a single, perfectly clear, and fully equitable consonance" (p. 3). And to show that this unification of law is feasible he argues (p. 5) that "not only is there no impediment, but the identical origin of our individual customs as well as their conformity in general principles make it manifestly clear that we can have a single custom."

aspect of this scientific interest in customary law was the sharpening and deepening of doubts which had already been accumulating as to the intellectual authority of Roman Law and its exclusive use in legal education. It was now apparent that much of Roman Law was irrelevant to French experience or even in conflict with its tendencies. And there was now a group of academic jurists who were no longer willing to assume, as in the past, that all such disagreements or discrepancies must be automatically resolved, in principle at least, against the customary law.[10] Limitations in the Roman Law had already been established by the work of the philologists and systematists. And under these conditions the sense of disagreement between French and Roman Law became an invitation and occasion to question the value of the latter as a universal code and to search for new theoretical foundations.

Critical attitudes, moreover, were similarly promoted by the appeal to French experience as an argument in public law. Such, for instance, was the invocation of custom by the Huguenots in their resistance to the Valois monarchy. As the alliance of a religious minority with a feudal opposition, the Huguenot party made a last defense of medieval constitutionalism against the absolutist conception of the monarchy. And the rights of the representative bodies, the chartered towns, and the local magnates on which the Huguenots depended for political support were ideologically defended by an explicit assertion of the customary principle against the theories derived from Roman Law. In

---

10 The position of the later middle ages is described by Declareuil, *Histoire générale du droit français,* p. 833, as follows: "La jurisprudence et la doctrine ont si fortement incliné les coutumes vers le droit romain qu'on en classe les dispositions en deux catégories: celles qui sont conformés au droit écrit et qui sont considérées, pour ce motif, comme de droit commun, et les autres, 'haineux de droict' ou de 'droict haineux' qu'on tient pour être de droit étroit, c'est-à-dire ne devant être étendues ni par analogue, ni d'une coutume à une autre."

Hotman, for example, this connection is extremely clear. One of the most savage of Huguenot polemicists, he was also the most militant of the anti-Romanists. And his *Franco-Gallia* is a rationalization of the medieval constitution which depends upon the systematic invocation of the customary principle.

Hotman, however, was exceptional. Although many of the great lawyers of the sixteenth century were either Protestants or sympathizers, their political doctrines were little shaped by Huguenot objectives. Bodin, a religious liberal with Protestant leanings,[11] aimed to strengthen the monarchy by refuting the right of resistance asserted by the Huguenots.[12] Du Moulin, a Protestant and the leading exponent of the customary law, interpreted the law of fiefs to enhance the powers of the crown.[13] For the class of magistrates and lawyers, in other words, mere religious sympathies could not alter a tradition of attachment to the monarchy which went back to the great era of the medieval legists. Their own position was much better represented by the party of the *Politiques*, of which, indeed, they were the main intellectual support.

[11] Bodin's interest in Protestantism was especially strong in the 1560s, as is indicated by his letter to Bautru of 1562. Later, Bodin developed his own theory of natural religion which breaks with Christianity completely. Throughout his life, however, he remained a Catholic outwardly. The only possible exception is a brief residence (and conversion) at Geneva in the 1550s, the evidence for which, although strong, is not incontestable.

[12] A major theme in *The Six Books of the Commonwealth* and one of the explicit intentions stated in its preface: "Il y en a d'autres contraires, et droits ennemis de ceux cy (the tyrant-princes), qui ne sont pas moins, et peut estre plus dangereux, qui soubs voile d'une exemption de charges, et liberté populaire, font rebeller les sugets contre leurs Princes naturels, ouvrant la porte à une licentieuse anarchie, qui est pire que la plus forte tyrannie du monde." Jean Bodin, *Six livres de la république*, preface.

[13] In his commentary on the customary law of Paris, under the title *De Feudis*. See Aubépin, "De l'influence de Dumoulin sur la législation française," *Revue critique de législation et de jurisprudence*, III, 608–25.

In the opinion of the *Politiques* the only solution to
the Civil Wars was to enhance the power of the monarchy
and to make it independent of religious factions.[14] They
did not assume, however, that reenforcement of the royal
power meant a sacrifice of vested legal rights of which, as
magistrates and lawyers, they felt themselves the cham-
pions. Unlike the Huguenots, they did not acknowledge
any basic conflict between the absolute power of the
crown and the security of local liberties. The royal power
seemed a guarantee of liberties because it was a guarantee
of the legal order which comprised them. There was held
to be a historic bond between Frenchmen and their kings
in which freedom and authority were reconciled. The deepest vision of the *Politiques*, accordingly, was a monarchy
absolute in principle in order to maintain the peace, but
reconciled to the liberties of Frenchmen by the advisory
check of the magisterial elite.

But this idea of a *monarchie temperée*, absolute and
limited at once, was difficult to formulate in the terms of
Roman public law, for the "original" *princeps* of the
Corpus Juris, as rediscovered by the humanists and applied
to France by enthusiasts for absolutism,[15] was the model of

---

[14] This is the conception which underlay their celebrated policy of
religious toleration. It was not, at least in L'Hospital, a principled defense of conscience. Persecution was repudiated because its effects were
politically ruinous. It compromised the independence of the monarchy
by making the crown the plaything of an extremist Catholic faction,
and it endangered the crown's prestige by unnecessary provocation of
the local powers. Toleration was therefore *politique*.

[15] During the heyday of Valois popularity under Francis I and Henry
II remarkable claims had sometimes been advanced. De Grassaille, for
example, had directly identified the constitutional powers of the king of
France with those of the ancient Roman emperors. And this was com-
bined with a notion of divine right which anticipated Bossuet. "The
king of France," said de Grassaille, "in his kingdom is like God incar-
nate. . . . For what the king does, he does as God and not himself. . . .
God speaks through the prince's mouth. . . . And he is *lex animata* in

a despot whose will could have no limit in the law. From Seyssel to Bodin,[16] accordingly, the conviction grew that the monarchy of France was a peculiar and indigenous creation; and the *Politiques*, quite as much as the Huguenots, appealed to this experience as a valid test of the principles of statecraft. The corresponding premise, in the realm of legal theory, was the conclusion of the universalists that the principles of public law were not to be taken from the Roman Law alone, but also from the legal and political experience of the French as well as other peoples.

The beginnings, at least, of a comparative approach to jurisprudence are already to be found in Baudouin's work of 1561. His *Prolegomenon on the Teaching of Universal History and Its Conjunction with Jurisprudence* is, for the most part, a long oration on the value and the method of historical studies. But the most important point, for present purposes, is that it was written by an academic jurist whose invitation to the study of universal history was linked with a critical reaction to conditions in his own profession. Baudouin's first and main complaint is that the traditional curriculum, oriented to the private law, is too narrow for the training of a jurisconsult. A jurisconsult, in the highest sense, must be prepared to give advice upon affairs of state.[17] And his art, the art of gov-

---

the land." Latin quoted in William Farr Church, *Constitutional Thought in Sixteenth-Century France*, p. 47, n. 10; translation mine.

[16] Claude de Seyssel's *La Grande monarchie de France* (1519) was an early attempt to formulate the idea of a moderate absolutism which was taken over by the *Politiques*. Seyssel, however, relies on the irrelevant, but highly popular, theory of the mixed state to explain the balance of the French monarchy.

[17] After speaking of the great jurist-historians of antiquity, Baudouin goes on to point the moral for contemporaries: "But who would not hope for even more from the many great men who flourish in this century? It is my wish, indeed, that the seed of men like these should not die out, and I especially desire that a school of civil studies should be opened from which men of prudence might go forth trained not only

erning, depends more upon the public law than on the private, which is useful mainly for the art of litigation. Second, the law schools do not even teach the private law correctly because they wrongly assume that their sources are complete and perfect. Parts of Roman Law and custom are not included in the *Corpus Juris*,[18] and many of those which are included cannot be understood as they are given, but must be interpreted from other sources.[19] And even then the law is not a single whole because the fragments of the *Corpus Juris* refer to different, and often incompatible strata of a long historical development.[20] The attempt, therefore, to teach the *Corpus Juris* as a system leads only to the invention of insoluble riddles on which the time of students is fruitlessly consumed, all the more fruitlessly, indeed, since much of what they learn cannot be practiced. From the viewpoint of domestic needs, parts of Roman Law are quite irrelevant.[21]

The traditional instruction is therefore insufficient. "Indeed," says Baudouin, "if there be any persuasion in my

---

for the private jurisdiction but for the greater faculty of fostering the commonwealth and for the governance of empires." *De institutione historiae universae et ejus cum jurisprudentia conjunctione prolegomenon*, p. 248. "But if it [the public law] is to be expounded, as it indeed it ought to be, should not history be called on first of all?" *Ibid.*, p. 249.

[18] "In the books of Justinian many things have been passed over which yet are clearly pertinent for jurisprudence." *Ibid.*, p. 211.

[19] "Who will deny that these fragments must be estimated first of all in terms of their origin and circumstances and that their understanding depends primarily on this?" *Ibid.*, p. 208.

[20] "That *Corpus Juris* (as it is called) which Justinian leaves us, is drawn from that great variety of Roman laws which are scattered over the thirteen hundred years from Romulus to Justinian. And not only are the old, the new, and the middle jurisprudence said to be of different kinds, but, having been almost annually changed, the condition of these laws is such that it is even a law that the later overrides the earlier. What else is there to do, accordingly, but to derive the order of their times from history, and keep, as it were, to some chronology of laws?" *Ibid.*, pp. 208–9. See above the statement of Budé, p. 22.

[21] Baudouin, *De institutione historiae universae*, p. 249.

words, or any outcome to my pleas, I should seek, entreat, and importune that those whose charge it is to take care that the commonwealth be not harmed should somehow, somewhere, rescue our youth from the thorny thickets of useless disputations, from that ivory tower school of idle dispositions—or, better still, from those fearful dungeons—and introduce them to a better course of study. . . . Time enough and labor has been spent, and mostly wasted, in unraveling twisted enigmas (I restrain myself from sharper language). Why are these things, nonsensical trifles I almost said, given more attention than the pleasant studies and literary masterpieces which I am praising in this work?" [22]

What law is lacking, history alone supplies: the proper context, first of all, as well as missing elements of law—a use of history which is reminiscent of Budé's. Second, and more importantly, history teaches the patterns and causes of revolutions in the form of states [23] and therewith the prudence required of a statesman. But instructive examples, holds Baudouin, are not confined to any single time or place, and history reveals its secrets only if it is understood as universal history.[24] Whatever, then, may be the case in private law, the Roman sources are not enough for statecraft. Can a pious Christian neglect the Hebrew commonwealth for which God himself was legislator? [25] Even if piety permitted, could he ignore ecclesiastical history, when the religious life of a people is obviously inseparably connected with their public law? [26] And shall the prej-

---

[22] *Ibid.*, pp. 252–53.   [23] *Ibid.*, p. 7.

[24] This point is made at length *ibid.*, pp. 37 ff. History can be understood only if its scattered parts are treated together (p. 38), if the chronological scheme is carried back to the very beginning (p. 44), etc. Baudouin, in a term surprisingly anticipatory of the nineteenth century, even speaks of history as "naturalem quandam individuitatem" (p. 47).

[25] *Ibid.*, pp. 65 ff.

[26] "But is the condition of the church sufficiently expounded, if one does not describe the commonwealth in whose bosom, as it were, the church is nourished? And again, is the body of the commonwealth suffi-

udices of a precious humanism persuade contemporaries
to dismiss the histories of European peoples as a mere
wilderness of Gothic barbarism? [27] This would be a reasonable omission if history were but an exercise in rhetoric.
But it deals with deeds, not words. The jurisconsult, accordingly, who does not know his origins, is wanting both
in piety and competence. "Base it is (says our Mucius) to
know nothing of the law in which we dwell. But baser still
by far to seem like strangers in our country and our
home." [28] "If we are Frenchmen, Britons, Germans, Spaniards, or Italians, and if we are to be able to speak of what
is ours, it is necessary that we do not ignore the history of
the Franks, Angles, Saxons, Goths, and Lombards; and
since our affairs are often confluent with theirs, we
may not remain ignorant of Saracen or Turkish history
either." [29]

One could easily infer from all of this that the Roman
Law, and perhaps the private quite as much as the public,
must be considered as but one component of a more universal field of legal or political experience from which
jurisprudence must be reconstructed. In his idea of a conjunction of history and law Baudouin comes very close to
this indeed. The law, he tells us, is itself a kind of history,
a selection from the record of the past which may be
reconnected to the whole. History, on the other hand, is
somewhat different from the law because the good and
bad in it are mixed together. And yet, if it is read with
standards of the lawyer, it may be taken as a source of
legal rules. The *Corpus* of history, therefore, stands beside
the *Corpus* of the law as a supplementary source of

---

ciently described, if one does not know the church which is its spirit,
as it were, and which is included in it, as I said?" *Ibid.*, p. 51.

[27] "I am aware that most of those who wish to be considered cultivated are willing students of the erudite histories of ancient times, but
fastidiously shrink back from the knowledge of more recent times which
they judge to be horrid and barbaric." *Ibid.*, p. 56.

[28] *Ibid.*, p. 59. [29] *Ibid.*, p. 63.

right.[30] Baudouin's greatest hope is that they may be fused into a single volume. "I should like," he says, "to see universal history assembled—sacred and civil, the old and the new, our own and that of foreigners; and at the same time a consolidation of jurisprudence also—the earlier and the later, the divine and the human. And then out of these two *corpora*, so to speak, of history and jurisprudence, I should like a single volume to be made." [31]

In Baudouin, however, this suggestion remains vague and undeveloped. The conjunction of history and jurisprudence is never quite identified with a comparative approach to law. Jurisprudence, generally speaking, is still equated with the study of the Roman civil law, although its outlines as a system have been all but lost in Roman history. And the lessons to be drawn from historical comparisons are considered more as a supplement to jurisprudence than as the basis of a new approach. With Bodin and Hotman, on the other hand, the appeal to history goes hand in hand with a principled rejection of a purely Romanistic jurisprudence. And the *locus classicus* of this attack is Hotman's *Antitribonianus* composed in 1567.

"The learned men of every age," says Hotman at the very beginning of his work, "have observed and voiced approval of the rule that the laws should be accommodated to the form and condition of the commonwealth, not the commonwealth to the laws." [32] For commonwealths which differ in their form, different laws will be required. What may consist with and preserve a democratic state or aris-

---

[30] "Indeed, the more we ask why this conjunction is desired, the more we shall understand that it is necessary precisely in the sense that the undivided parts or members of a single body neither can nor ought to be disjoined. I, indeed, have not yet been able to decide whether history receives more light from the books of jurisprudence, or jurisprudence from the monuments of history." *Ibid.,* p. 178.

[31] *Ibid.,* pp. 210–11.   [32] Hotman, *Antitribonianus,* p. 139.

tocracy may be irrelevant, or even subversive, in a monarchy. Even where states are similar in form they may
differ in their special circumstances. One monarchy may
be larger than another, or more despotic, or more milita-
ristic, "and consequently, the laws of one monarchy are
often useless to another, just as medicines are not all suit-
able to all men whatsoever without consideration of their
sex, their age, and nationality." [33] With Hotman, therefore,
the historical circumstances of a commonwealth are established as the test of legislation. And the ground has thus
been won to pose the fateful and unprecedented question
as to the relevance of Roman Law. "This principle being
posited," continues Hotman, "we must consider the two
parts of civil law . . . so that when both of them have been
expounded we may judge whether the books of Justinian
are of any special value for the state of France." [34]

The first stage of his polemic, accordingly, is to multiply
examples from contemporary practice to show that Roman
Law is so divergent from the law of France as to be all but
completely "out of use." [35] In the realm of public law, to
begin with, the entire Roman system is pivoted on the
division of the citizen body into the two classes of patricians and plebeians. French law, however, depends upon a
threefold scheme of nobles, roturiers, and serfs.[36] As to
magistrates, the Roman forms are so ill reported in the
Corpus Juris, and were so often changed, that they are
hardly capable of definite comparison. Nevertheless, it is
obvious that no counterpart exists in France to the consuls
of the classical republic, to take only a single fundamental
instance. The Roman consul was a popularly elected mag-

---

[33] *Ibid.,* p. 141.   [34] *Ibid.,* p. 140.
[35] Hotman, as he tells us in his preface (*ibid.,* p. 138), divides his
polemic into two main parts. The first is an attack upon the relevance
of Roman Law; the second an attack on its assumed perfection.
[36] *Ibid.,* p. 143.

istrate whose functions were primarily executive. The only parallel in France, if such it may be called, would be the royal privy council.[37] Even if comparison be restricted to the later period of Roman history when the form of the commonwealth was roughly similar to the monarchy of France, the divergencies are no less great. For this period many magistracies mentioned by the *Corpus Juris* are but a list of esoteric names whose functions are clearly obsolete: the *Praefectus Urbi, Praefectus Augustalis, Procurator Caesaris, Praesides or Proconsul provinciae,* the *legati* of these, or their *vicem obtinentes,* the *Praefectus Praetorio Africae, Magister militum, Magister officiorum, Comes sacrarum largitionum, Comes rerum privatarum, Comes sacri patrimonii,* the *rector* of Pannonia, Pisidia, and a list of other provinces.[38]

"Who," asks Hotman, "will not judge the man deranged who would spend his entire life in working out the duties, instructions, and concepts of such magistrates, in order to adapt them to our France, when we are so different from these nations in our character and customs? I shall put it briefly. If we are preparing a young man for some service to the commonwealth of France, let us consider to which of the two studies he ought rather to apply himself, whether he should learn about the magistrates of Rome or Constantinople, or the ministers of the crown and of the law courts of this kingdom—for example, whether he should understand the sovereign powers of the kingship; the power and authority of the three estates; the right of the queen, the dauphin, and the brothers of the king and their appanages; the right of the princes, the royal bastards, the royal brothers, the constable, the peers, the marshals of France, the masters of the royal chamber, the admiral, the

[37] *Ibid.,* pp. 144-45.   [38] *Ibid.,* p. 145.

dukes, counts, viscounts, adjutants, barons; and likewise
the functions of the treasurers of France, the praefects of
the fisc and of supplies; and in judicial matters the functions of the chancellor, privy counsellor, *maîtres des re-
quêtes*, parlement, bailiffs, seneschals." [39]

These divergencies, although not grounded in a systematic theory nor exhaustively developed or explained, are
enough for Hotman to conclude that "as to things pertaining to the commonwealth, the study of the Roman state
can be of no value to the government of France, because
the forms of these two commonwealths are not in any way
alike." [40]

Even more extensive, and more damaging, is Hotman's
analysis of private law, where the Roman sources had
been deemed to be most clearly universal. A good example
of his treatment is the Roman law on the state of persons,
which is built on the division between free and servile in-
dividuals. The study of the modes by which free status is
acquired presents the contemporary jurist with a whole
variety of types of manumission, of actions and officials
by which these may be executed, and of diverse degrees of
citizenship to which manumission may give rise—all of
which are manifestly adapted to very special Roman circumstances. Certain forms of inferior status, moreover, in-
volve principles which are morally objectionable. Infanti-
cide, the unlimited power of the father over his children,
the sale of the woman, mere cohabitation as the source of
marital obligation, and certain aspects of illegitimacy are
laws of pagan inspiration which no Christian jurist may
accept.[41]

Of these very special or objectionable laws, some at least
had become mere fictions in the course of time, and others
were specifically abolished or amended by the later em-

[39] *Ibid.*, p. 146.   [40] *Ibid.*, p. 148.   [41] *Antitribonianus*, pp. 149–50.

perors. But, nevertheless, they are so deeply rooted in the
legal system that the contemporary jurist still must give
them careful study. A nice illustration of the way in which
"all the books of Tribonian are erected on these things" [42]
occurs in Hotman's treatment of the Roman law on the
qualities of things. The basic distinction between property
acquired according to the special procedures of the ancient
jus civile (*res mancipi*) and that acquired by the ordinary
forms of contract reflects, says Hotman, the original pri-
vileges of native Romans over neighboring or allied
peoples.[43] The political point of this distinction became
obscure with the expansion of the empire, and its basis dis-
appeared entirely when the citizenship of Rome was universally conceded to her subjects. Yet it was so woven into
the very fabric of the law that it could not even be abolished when the seat of empire was removed to Constantinople. What absurdity, then, to pore over legal institutions
which even the Romans felt were obsolete! "Nevertheless,
it is acknowledged by the most celebrated doctors that
without this knowledge the *Digest* is completely unintelligible." [44]

This analysis is carried out for every division of the
Roman private law, which finally appears, on every level
and in every area, to be permeated by the circumstances
peculiar to its history. At every point Hotman goes to
contemporary practice, and to customary law especially,
to draw example after example in which French institutions
are not only divergent from the Roman Law, but do not

---

[42] *Ibid.*, p. 152.

[43] "In the first place, there is the division of things into *res mancipi*
and *non mancipi* which was of great force and moment between Roman
citizens. There is no doubt that this distinction was invented by them
as a special privilege and prerogative of Roman citizens over those of
neighbouring and allied states." *Ibid.*, p. 155.

[44] *Ibid.*, p. 157.

even seem to have a counterpart.[45] His conclusion, therefore, is the same for private law as public. "Let it be
judged," says Hotman in one of his innumerable polemical
asides, "what the youth of France should say to those who
have led them to expend their time on things like these
[the Roman Law] which have neither utility nor application, and are, as in a saying of Justinian, nothing if not
ancient fables. Indeed, it is almost as if our priests and
monks were to teach their novices to jump and leap in
solemn prayer because once upon a time the Roman Salii
used to do the same." [46]

But although Hotman, in these extreme polemical flights,
seems to be rejecting Roman Law *in toto*, he was too good
a lawyer and a humanist to believe his own exaggerations.
Roman legal institutions had deeply affected practice, and
even where practice was divergent the general categories
of Roman jurisprudence were the basis of interpretation.
As to the humanist opinion that there was a special legal
virtue in the Romans, Hotman is willing to "admit and to
confess" that "if there was ever a commonwealth fertile
in this art and discipline, it was the Roman." [47] Hotman's
real intention, we shall see, was the *selective* use of Roman
models.[48] The target of his wrath is not the Roman influence in general, but the assumption that the Roman Law,
as embodied in the *Corpus Juris*, must be studied in every
jot and tittle as a universal code. The second phase of his
polemic, therefore, is an attempt to prove that the *Corpus*

[45] Thus in his discussion of the "status of persons," Hotman mentions
the three estates of France, the rights of lords and vassals, the various
forms of serfdom, and the distinction between natural and other subjects
of the French crown. For all of these the Roman law is held to be of
little use. As to the three estates, for instance, the Roman distinction
between patricians and plebeians "contains nothing comparable to these.
Nor is there any mention of these things in the books of Tribonian."
Ibid., p. 153.
[46] *Ibid.*, p. 154.　　　[47] *Ibid.*, p. 137.　　　[48] See below, p. 56.

Juris, far from giving us the best of Roman legal wisdom, distorts it through juridical incompetence.

The *Corpus Juris*, to begin with, is held to be inconsistent in its elements. The sixteenth century had reconstructed Roman legal history and was increasingly aware that the law had changed with circumstances. After every revolution in their state, shows Hotman, the Romans made drastic alterations in their institutions.[49] And even where the forms remained unchanged their content often varied greatly. "When the Roman *Imperium* was removed to Constantinople, what remained the same in its magistrates and provincial governors, beyond the name and title?"[50] In the time of Justinian, accordingly, there was an unwieldy mass of laws which often stemmed from unrelated or inconsistent principles.[51] And since Tribonian, in Hotman's judgment, lacked the art and the knowledge to order this material, the *Corpus Juris* is full of insoluble antinomies.

Even worse, the *Corpus Juris* is a weak and treacherous guide to the realities of Roman institutions. Tribonian, to begin with, denies us the necessary sources. The most famous Roman legislation—the laws of the people, the praetorian edicts, and the senatorial decrees—are not reported in the words of the original.[52] They are represented

---

[49] *Antitribonianus*, pp. 139–40. The discussion is introduced as follows: "And when any commonwealth has changed its form, it has changed its laws and statutes at the same time. An example is provided in the history of Rome." The history of Roman Law is thus the prime example of the tendency of law to change with circumstances.

[50] *Ibid.*, pp. 141–42.

[51] "As far as the contents are concerned, in his century there were an infinite number of laws in the Roman state. . . . And in view of the variation in the course of time, and the different forms of the commonwealth (to which we have referred at the beginning) they were frequently in conflict with each other, and one repealed another." *Ibid.*, p. 181. Hotman goes on (pp. 181–82) to add that the confusion of the laws was further promoted by elaboration of the laws in commentaries.

[52] *Ibid.*, p. 186.

by commentaries only, which seem to remove us from reality. "Or is there anyone who holds the gracious muses in such low esteem, or is so much a foe of nature, as to be content with the commentaries of a Eustathius or Servius in place of the writings of a Homer or a Vergil?" [53] Of commentaries, moreover, we do not even have the best. The two Catos, Mucius and Servius Sulpitius—these were jurists who flourished at the peak of Roman virtue. In the *Corpus Juris*, their work does not appear. In their stead we are offered only epigones—Africanus, Triphoninus, Modestinus, Javolenus—whose very names betray provincial origins. Could men whose native tongue was usually Greek, and who learned Latin as a second language, have really understood the sources when Cicero, writing in an earlier and better age, already laments the obscurity of these? [54] In this process of selection, furthermore, the wisdom of the Romans is perverted by inclusions as well as by omissions. If the laws and writers of the greatest age are slighted, the rescripts of the later emperors are represented in all too great abundance. "Here," says Hotman, "I leave it to anyone of sound and healthy judgment to consider how much equity is to be found in these rescripts of infamous tyrants, who more rightly deserve the name of abominable and devilish monsters than that of Roman emperors." [55]

Finally, of these defective sources all we get from Tribonian are excerpts. Such mutilated fragments are these that the institutions they report are stultified.[56] Ask a contemporary student about the functions of a Roman magistrate, and what kind of nonsense does one hear? "Consuls, acting alone and individually, may grant a manumission,

---

[53] *Ibid.*, p. 187.   [54] *Ibid.*, pp. 185, 187–88.   [55] *Ibid.*, pp. 182–83.

[56] "In this entire congeries he has not given us an entire discourse, but rather interrupted speeches pieced together from many different places, sometimes from one author, sometimes from another, without any link or thread of argument." *Ibid.*, p. 190.

but someone who has put his cause before one of them may not ask manumission of the other." [57] This, implicitly, is Hotman's answer to the systematists' claim that the *Corpus Juris* was entire in its contents. The fragments, furthermore, are colored in their meaning by the context given by Justinian's commissioners. And not only the spirit of the sources but their letter also is of doubtful authenticity. Tribonian claims that he has added nothing of his own. From him, however, come the titles and summations which often replace verbatim reproduction. With the rediscovery of certain sources Tribonian even stands convicted not only of amending the wording of the fragments but of inserting whole sentences and pages.[58]

Through all of this, the constantly reiterated point is that the *Corpus Juris* is not the "Roman" law, but the specific product of the age of Justinian which, for Hotman and the century of humanism, was the nadir of the classic virtues. The Roman state had been shattered, and the monuments of Roman statecraft lay strewn about in ruins. The men who selected and collated them were Graeculi and Byzantines, who were estranged from the Roman spirit by nation, place, and time. As to their juristic skill, what can we expect, asks Hotman, from an age in which "all good letters and instruction had been undoubtedly extinguished in Greece, and Roman jurisprudence had been utterly buried beneath a veritable Gothic flood." [59] As to the mo-

---

[57] *Ibid.*, p. 147.

[58] *Ibid.*, pp. 191–92. The source to which Hotman especially refers is Paul's *Sentences* which had been rediscovered some thirty years before. In general, says Hotman, "after good letters opened the ears and minds of men, not long ago, it was discovered that Tribonian had added not only two or three words of his own, but whole lines and sentences, and even pages. . . ." *Ibid.*, p. 192. On the detection of interpolations, see Finetti, *Storia della ricerca delle interpolazioni nel Corpus Juris Giustineaneo*.

[59] *Antitribonianus*, p. 185.

rality of Justinian and Tribonian, he is willing to credit the most scurrilous gossip to prove that Roman virtue had utterly degenerated.[60] Had we not the *Corpus Juris* before us to confirm the worst, asks Hotman, "what might we have expected from the undertaking of such a man, in so unfortunate an age, in so vast a multitude of books, amidst so great a confusion of the laws, with such associates, and in so brief a space of time?" [61] The *Corpus Juris*, his whole analysis responds, is nothing but the testament of decadence.

But if the *Corpus Juris* is a mere fragment of the Roman law, and does not even represent the best of it, then all the labors on its study have been wasted. Hotman's summation of the "modes of teaching" is designed to show that the modern method is no more certain than the medieval, that each produces its own variety of futile disputations because the source itself is inherently inadequate.[62] To the extent, therefore, that the legal wisdom of the Romans is of value,

[60] *Ibid.*, pp. 184–85. Suidas is cited to the effect that Tribonian was a pagan, a sycophant, and a scoundrel. Procopius reports that he used his commission to sell justice in the market place, and twisted the law to fit the wishes of the highest bidder. Evagrius and Zonaras call Justinian an avaricious tyrant. That such scandal was widely credited in the sixteenth century is indicated by a corresponding passage in Rabelais which occurs at the end of his story about Bridlegoose. "What made the abuse even more glaring was that their jurisdiction was ruled by Tribonian, an evil, perfidious barbarian; a man so corrupt, malign, and iniquitous as to sell laws, edicts, bills, constitutions and ordinances at public auction, cash down, to the highest bidder. Piece by piece, scrap by scrap, Tribonian had drawn up their mince-meat code, suppressing and abolishing the whole law, the meat and body and spirit of right. For he feared that the latter might remain permanent, like the work of ancient jurisconsults, as immortalized in the Twelve Tables and the Praetorian edicts. This would have exposed to the entire world his dishonesty and baseness." *The Five Books of Gargantua and Pantagruel*, Bk. III, ch. XLIV, p. 458.

[61] *Antitribonianus*, p. 186.

[62] "For we are talking not of the common disputes which began some forty or fifty years ago against the sophistic arts of the barbarians, but of a natural vice which inheres in the material and substance of this discipline, and which is far more difficult to correct than corruptions which have arisen extrinsically and by accident." *Ibid.*, p. 210.

it is better learned from their historians than from a study of the *Corpus Juris*. "Who does not know," asks Hotman, "that one can learn more about the Roman magistrates from one year's reading of the Greek and Latin historians —and with far more delight and ease—than in the whole six years of study on these fragments and snatches left over in the books of Justinian?" [63]

Thus the *Corpus Juris*, our polemicist would have it, is contradictory, confused, fragmentary, and "out of use" to boot.[64] However much these assertions are exaggerated, their implications, nonetheless, are of great theoretical significance. The historical and logical criticisms implicit in the *mos docendi Gallicus* have now been carried to the breaking point. By the tests of history and logic the *Corpus Juris* has been exposed as something less than complete or universal. It does not embody all of Roman legal wisdom and is often irrelevant to European needs. This conclusion is not affected by Hotman's polemical inaccuracies. He could have said far less and still have established the essential point.

The final issue, then, as Hotman understands it, is the creation of a new and simple legal code by an appeal to reason and experience. To this end, the Chancellor l'Hospital, that "Solon" of the French, is entreated to appoint a "new commission" [65]—the very term bespeaks defiance of Justinian—which is to look upon the *Corpus Juris* not as an ultimate authority but as a "treasury" of legal wisdom from which things of value may be borrowed as seems fit.[66] In

---

[63] *Ibid.*, p. 146.

[64] "The greatest part is either repealed and obsolete, or full of disorder and confusion, or packed with contradictions and antinomies, or infected with corruptions and mistakes, or thrown into doubt and controversy by corrections and alterations since these are made in such great number." *Ibid.*, p. 208.

[65] *Ibid.*, p. 215.

[66] "In which [the *Corpus Juris*] they will be able to find things of

the construction of a code, accordingly, the opinions of philosophers should also be consulted, together with practical experience and, of great importance to a Christian commonwealth, the old Mosaic law in so far as it was not peculiar to the Jewish state and abrogated by the advent of Christianity. In this purification the Mosaic law is to be measured by the law of nature.[67] The essential theme, in any case, is that this borrowing of rules and principles must be a process of critical selection. Such questions, for example, as the liberty of testament, or the principle and terms of primogeniture—on which French and Roman customs differ—are now to be settled by equity, not exegesis, by the free exercise of human reason and not, as in the past, by "the vain minutiae of words and syllables." [68] And the equitable solutions thus discovered are to be adapted to the special needs of France by a consideration of her form of state.[69]

What Hotman is anticipating, therefore, is a final movement of juristic thought from the exegesis of authority to a general theory of law and legislation. But this remains anticipation, and no more, since the brief suggestions of his concluding chapter are on the level of mere practical proposals without clear theoretical direction. The general invocation of "reason" and "experience" is less the specifica-

excellence and beauty, and which will truly be a treasury of inestimable value. . . ." *Ibid.*, p. 215.

[67] The commissioners are not to select "things which concern the state, form, and governance of the Jewish commonwealth (which have clearly been repealed by the coming of Jesus Christ) but only those which gleam with rectitude, reason, and natural equity, by which all human beings are bound—those who lived before, as well as those who lived after Moses—and which the ancient pagans called the law of nature, or the law of nations or peoples." *Ibid.*, p. 216.

[68] *Ibid.*, p. 219.

[69] "And in this matter [of a code] let them [the commissioners] follow the law of Justinian where it seems convenient, and let them refer everything to the state and form of the commonwealth (as we said at the beginning)." *Ibid.*, p. 217.

tion of a method than an invitation to discover one. And although there are certain hints of a historical and comparative approach, all actual questions of procedure are handed over, as it were, to the future members of his new commission. Hotman's contribution, therefore, is essentially restricted to a clearing of the ground, to a polemical negation of traditional authority. And it is only with the work of Jean Bodin that an actual attempt is made to reconstruct juristic science on a base of universal history.

IV

JEAN BODIN AND
THE COMPARATIVE APPROACH TO
UNIVERSAL JURISPRUDENCE

Although the goal of universal synthesis inspires all of Bodin's work on law, and is the key to its most general significance, the motivations and background of his project are not extensively discussed in any of his extant writings.[1] Nevertheless, the traces of Bodin's development are unmistakably recorded in an *Oration* he delivered at Toulouse (1559), in his early sketch of systematic jurisprudence entitled *Juris universi distributio* (about 1559), in the preface to the *Methodus* (1566), and in a preface to the *Juris universi distributio* which may have been written after 1566. And since these rather cryptic indications[2] are often

---

[1] Before his death in 1596, Bodin ordered burned, in his presence, his *De Imperio, De jurisdictione, De legis actionibus, De decretis,* and *De judiciis.* These seem to have been a series of monographic manuscripts on Roman public law dating from his Toulousan period. They were burned, undoubtedly, because Bodin felt his position on public law to be better represented by *The Six Books of the Commonwealth.* Yet these products of his law school days must have contained references to then raging methodological disputes which would have enhanced our knowledge of his intellectual development. The report of the burning of these manuscripts is from Ménage, *Réflexions sur la vie de Pierre Ayrault* (Paris, 1658), according to Roger Chauviré, *Jean Bodin, Auteur de la République,* p. 95.

[2] In the prefaces especially, where Bodin is most far-ranging in his declarations, it must be remembered that he is addressing friends or patrons who are familiar with contemporary issues. The chatty style requires no systematic exposition.

misinterpreted or missed, a brief summation may be useful in order to demonstrate that the entire basis of his major works was a very early and permanent commitment to the deepest problems of the *mos docendi Gallicus*.

That Bodin's earliest ideas were humanist may be inferred from the fact that he entered the Law School at Toulouse in the later 1540s when the reforms of Budé and Alciato had been widely introduced. Toulouse, perhaps, was more conservative than Bourges.[3] But even so there would never have been any question of his humanist beginnings if not for the story, long accredited, of a cabal against his "rival" Cujas which seems to indicate affinities to Bartolism. In the 1550s there was a bitter fight over a professorial appointment [4] at Toulouse in which, according to the story, Cujas was the hero of the humanists and Forcadel the candidate of Bartolist resistance. Bodin is supposed to have conspired with the forces of reaction and to have played a leading role in the victory of Forcadel.[5] Recent research, however, has given overwhelming proof that

[3] Toulouse was a center of orthodoxy in religion and law during the sixteenth century, and the law school was generally conservative except for a brief period from 1540 to 1560. See the magnificent reconstruction of the atmosphere in Pierre Mesnard, "Jean Bodin à Toulouse," *Bibliothèque d'humanisme et renaissance, travaux et documents*, XII (1950), 31–59.

[4] Since appointment, tenure, and salary were utterly erratic and depended exclusively on a man's reputation and popularity, the competition was savage and ferocious—even murderous, when it led to student riots, as it often did. This atmosphere helps to explain the demeaning nastiness of academic feuding in the sixteenth century, of which the insults exchanged between Cujas and Bodin later on are only a moderate example. Bodin himself gives some interesting information on the insecurities of the academic profession in his oration at Toulouse (*Oratio, Oeuvres philosophiques*, pp. 19B–20A), where he speaks of the sad fate of scholars forced to hire out as private tutors. A major complaint is that they have no time for research!

[5] For this version of the affair see Chauviré, *Jean Bodin*, pp. 28–29. The story is so constantly reported in earlier versions of Bodin's life that Chauviré is hardly to be blamed for having credited it.

there was not the slightest evidence of Bartolism in Bodin's early thinking or behavior. There was no conspiracy; Forcadel himself was not a Bartolist; Cujas was not yet famous as a humanist; Bodin was not his rival either personally or intellectually and, far from being involved in any plot, may not even have been present at the time! [6] The story is undoubtedly the fabrication of a later generation attempting to explain the feud between Cujas and Bodin which broke out after the publication of the *Commonwealth*. It was probably accepted and perpetuated by the Law School of Toulouse in order to have a scapegoat, in Bodin, for its own oversight in letting Cujas go.[7]

In any event, by the time of his *Oration to the Senate and People of Toulouse on the Education of the Youth of the Commonwealth*, which came in 1559 towards the end of his academic period, Bodin appears not only as an enthusiastic legal humanist but as one who has begun to explore the broadest implications of the movement. The aim of the address was to persuade the burghers of Toulouse to appropriate funds for a college of liberal arts on the model of the humanist *Collège de France*,[8] a project which Bodin defended by recounting the history and glories of the Renaissance and expounding a humanist theory of education. In the course of this defense he anticipated and an-

[6] Moreau-Reibel, *Jean Bodin*, pp. 8–15, refutes the story by showing that the Cujas-Bodin rivalry does not go back that far. Mesnard, "Jean Bodin à Toulouse," reconstructs the true situation. His conclusion: "Nous en avons assez dit, croyons-nous, pour prouver qu'il n'y a pas eu contre Cujas de complot Forcadel en 1554, a fortiori de complot Bodin pour le compte de Forcadel" (p. 51). As to Bodin, there is some evidence that he was in Geneva from 1552 to 1553 (I omit the details and pros and cons of the longish controversy on this point).

[7] Mesnard, "Jean Bodin à Toulouse," pp. 44–45.

[8] The proposal had already been approved and needed only to be executed. Bodin's interest was more than philosophic, for, like Cujas, he had failed to get a regular professorship at the Law School, and was apparently hoping that he might be named head of the humanist college. See Mesnard, "Jean Bodin à Toulouse," p. 51.

swered the objection that a humanist college would in-
culcate distaste for law, and further undermine the law
school, which had been losing students to competitors like
Bourges. It need no longer be assumed, he answered, that
a man can never be a jurisconsult unless he is a first-class
ignoramus and barbarian. "This foul and unbecoming blot,
which had too long stained the name of jurisconsults, has
been erased by Budé, has been erased by Alciato, has been
erased by Connan, and has been erased by many others
also. . . . " [9] It was, in fact, the crudities of medieval barbarism which had been driving students from Toulouse
by making the law repulsive to the young. Only the sweet
gardens of humanist instruction would serve to lure them
back. In this defense of legal humanism not only the senti-
ments, but the words as well, could have been taken directly from Budé.

Bodin, moreover, was already thinking of the need for
"system." *Jus in artem redigere* is an inevitable part of the
task of reconstructing jurisprudence, and the capacity for
"introducing system" has the final and climactic place in his
list of the virtues of the lawyer. The best of jurists, says
Bodin, are those "who have diligently traced the source
and root of law to its ultimate beginning; who have accurately rendered the entire history of legislators and jurisconsults together with the knowledge of antiquity; who
have clearly grasped the jurisdiction, power, and duties of
the Roman *princeps*, senate, people, and magistrates; who
have applied the books of philosophers on the laws, the
commonwealth, and the virtues to the interpretation of the
law; who have shown perfect knowledge of the Greek and
Latin languages in which the laws have been commanded
and described; who have clearly joined their precepts to
the writings of the law court and the council; and who,

[9] *Oratio, Oeuvres philosophiques*, pp. 17A–17B.

finally, have circumscribed the entire art [of law] within its boundaries, marked out its main divisions, distributed its parts, defined its terms, and provided illustrations." [10]

It will be noted, finally, that the systematic exposition demanded in the closing section is briefly outlined in the *Juris universi distributio.* Bodin's purpose here is a logical arrangement of the law in its entirety in accordance with the rules of Peter Ramus.[11] But he has now concluded that a truly general and comprehensive *distributio* cannot be achieved by an arrangement of the Roman law alone. In theory, at least, the basic components of his scheme are derived from the juridical experience of all of the most famous states. Moreover, although we have no edition of the *Juris universi distributio* which is earlier than 1578, it almost surely belongs to Bodin's academic or Toulousan period.[12] Hence by the age of twenty-nine or thirty he had already moved towards a universalist approach.

Six years later, when the preface to the *Methodus* was composed, Bodin had long since quit Toulouse. Bitterly disappointed in his academic hopes, he had come to Paris to practice as an advocate in *Parlement.* He now aspired to a royal counselorship and was politically involved with the faction of the *Politiques.* And it is often thought that corresponding to the change of fortune there was an important shift in intellectual direction. He expressed such venom now towards certain colleagues of his teaching days, such scorn for academic trivialities, and so much praise for "practice" and "experience" that he seemed to

---

[10] *Oratio, Oeuvres philosophiques,* pp. 17A–18B.

[11] For the influence of Ramus on Bodin, see Kenneth D. McRae, "Ramist Tendencies in the Work of Jean Bodin," *Journal of the History of Ideas,* XVI, 306–23.

[12] This is the opinion of John L. Brown, *The Methodus . . . of Jean Bodin,* pp. 25–26, and he is supported by Mesnard, *Oeuvres philosophiques de Jean Bodin,* p. 69.

have broken with the humanists and become, instead, a "neo-Bartolist." Indeed, in an often quoted passage from a later polemic against Cujas he seems to be stating this explicitly. "If," he says, "there is any mistake which merits forgiveness, I suppose that Cujas should be pardoned, for I am not ashamed to confess that once I shared his error. This was the time when I was teaching Roman Law at Toulouse, and in the circle of young men thought myself exceedingly wise. At that time I thought there was little or no wisdom in those princes of juristic science, in Bartolus, I say, Baldus, Alexander, Faber, Paulus, Du Moulin, and almost the whole order of judges and advocates. But after I was initiated into the secrets of jurisprudence in the law courts, and was confirmed in the daily experience of practical affairs, I came to understand at last that true and solid legal wisdom lay not in academic dust but in the battles of the courtroom, not in the weights of syllables but in the scales of equity and justice. I learned that those who know nothing of the practice of the courts languish in the profoundest ignorance of Roman law." [13]

Nevertheless, the image of Bodin the neo-Bartolist, although often encountered, is misleading. Bodin's respect for Bartolus and the commentators, his contempt for "jugglers of syllables," and his hostility to Cujas are not at all conclusive as evidence of a break with humanist perspectives. Alciato and Zasius had always insisted on some familiarity with the problems and solutions of the commentators in order to prepare the student for the application of the law in practice. Extremists, on the other hand, who regarded classical philology as the sole resource of legal education, had been regularly condemned by the more "practical" humanists as mere "grammarians" and

[13] Bodin, letter to Guy du Faur, seigneur de Pibrac (Vidus Faber), in *Six livres de la république* (1579).

"pedants," and Cujas, who is Bodin's target here, had become, justifiably or not, a favorite butt of such attacks.[14] Bodin's polemics, therefore, were not at all peculiar to the Bartolists but were characteristic themes of what might be called the moderate humanist position.[15]

The most convincing evidence, however, that Bodin remained consistent with his past is the writings of Bodin himself. His review of Romanistic jurisprudence, which is one of the subjects in his preface of 1566, proceeds from an attack on medieval "ignorance," and a defense of the humanist enlightenment, which is almost the same as that of the *Oratio*. Medieval law is still portrayed as a wilderness of rocks and thorns which has repelled the spirit of the young. The older commentators, Bodin adds, have produced such an abundance of confusion, as to make it seem that they spent all their time in writing, and none at all in reading. He is willing to concede that they may have done the best they could in view of the barbaric age in which they lived, but there is all the less reason, therefore, for the enlightened modern to continue in their footsteps.[16] In any event, the first accomplishment of contemporary jurisprudence is to have restored the "pristine dignity" of Roman Law, a process of purging medieval errors in which the humanist arts have been essential.[17] And if Bodin is contemptuous of certain humanists, it is not because he disapproves their goal but because they have been guilty

---

[14] For contemporary criticisms of the humanists see Alberico Gentili (Gentilis), *De iuris interpretibus dialogi sex*, ed. Guido Astuti (1937; original edition, 1582), Guido Astuti, *Mos italicus e mos gallicus nei dialoghi "De iuris interpretibus" di Alberico Gentili*, and Guido Kisch, *Humanismus und Jurisprudenz, Der Kampf zwischen mos italicus und mos gallicus an der Universität Basel*.

[15] As it might be represented, for example, by the position of Duaren. See Stintzing, *Geschichte der deutschen Rechtswissenschaft*, I, 369.

[16] *Methodus, Oeuvres philosophiques*, p. 108A.

[17] "But after they began to be thoroughly cleansed, the pristine dignity of the Roman laws seemed to have been restored." *Ibid.*

of excesses which defeat it. "For those who should gently
have cleansed the ancient tablets of their spots and blemishes,
so that the ancient picture could be recognized, have used
a steely pen, and have so deeply and indelibly etched their
vile notes on all the books, that the image of antiquity
scarcely can appear." [18] What better proof that Bodin's
indictment of the "academics" is directed exclusively at
"pure grammarians" like Cujas?

This same preface, to be sure, contains a fourfold classification and ranking of contemporary jurists in which there
is an emphasis on practical experience not present in his
earlier work.[19] But this is not in any sense a brute empiricism set up against the claims of theory. If the cloistered
academic à la Cujas is the first and worst of types, the mere
empiricist fares little better. Those who have picked up
prudence from the law courts only, are relegated to the
second class and passed over with barest mention. It is
only when we come to those in whom practice is com-
bined with precepts, says Bodin, that something of value
can be found.[20] This third class, indeed, contains all of
Bodin's favorite contemporaries—among them Baro, Connan, and Du Moulin ("the glory of our guild") the first
two of whom were famous academics. But even this is
not the ultimate, for there is yet another class of jurists
(the only member seems to be Bodin) in which philosophy
and literary culture are joined to precepts and experience.[21] The last and highest type of jurist, therefore, is the

18 *Methodus, Oeuvres philosophiques*, p. 109B.
19 In the *Oratio*, as we have seen, Bodin refers to the need for attend-
ing to the wisdom of the law courts, but he makes no special point of it.
See above, p. 62.
20 "The third class consists of those who have learned the practice
from the second, and precepts from the first. . . . From these we derive
many things useful for deciding and judging civil causes, from the others
almost nothing." *Methodus, Oeuvres philosophiques*, p. 108B.
21 "The final class consists of those who are educated not only in

one in which the theoretical and humanist elements are most pronounced. Indeed, Bodin is so fully consistent with his past that his description of this legal paragon is a repetition, almost word for word, of the universally cultivated jurist portrayed in his *Oration* at Toulouse.[22]

What has really happened in these years at Paris is a sharpening, and deepening, of Bodin's original commitment. He had already moved, as we have shown, from the Romanism of Budé and Alciato to the program of a universal synthesis, and now, his awareness heightened by experience, the goal of synthesis seemed all the more inevitable. The laws of France, he now points out, urgently require to be codified, and there are Papinians and Labeos enough if only they would break with the authority of Rome and create a system of their own.[23] In the teaching of the law, moreover, the lack of "art" or "system" is a scandal to the whole profession, but the academic jurists, he complains, in attempting to create a system, have confined themselves to the system of the Roman *jus civile* which, like the law of any other single state, is almost by definition peculiar and imperfect, at least in certain of its parts.[24] Thus for all of the reforms demanded by the age, in teaching as well as in practice, the sole remaining barrier is the traditional authority of Rome against which the attack now delivered by Bodin is in striking parallel to the polemics of the other anti-Romanists.

---

precepts and forensic practice, but in the foremost arts and sound philosophy. . . ." *Ibid.*

[22] *Ibid.*   [23] *Ibid.*, pp. 108B–109A.

[24] "Indeed, they [the systematizers of the Roman law] have been so far distant from the goal which they had postulated that they do not seem to understand what an art is. For the arts and sciences . . . are of universals, not particulars, but these men have attempted an art of *jus civile*, of the law, that is, of a single and specific commonwealth." *Ibid.*, p. 107B. Cf. *Juris universi distributio, Oeuvres philosophiques*, pp. 71A–71B.

I shall not mention [says Bodin] the absurdity of wishing to draw conclusions about universal law from the laws of Rome which were subject to unceasing change, especially since almost all the laws of the Twelve Tables were repealed by an infinite multitude of edicts and statutes and afterwards, indeed, by the Aebutian Rogation, and thereafter the old laws were repeatedly replaced by new ones springing up. We see, indeed, that Justinian's law has been almost entirely abrogated by succeeding emperors. And of those remaining, I refrain from saying how many are absurd, and how many have been rendered obsolete by the just decrees of almost all peoples, and by customary usage.[25]

What we have of Roman Law, moreover, has been distorted by the "figments of the *Graeculi.*"

For the fifteen men, commissioned by Justinian to codify the laws at a time when everything was overwhelmed by monstrous barbarism, have left the legal sources so confused that almost nothing pure can be extracted from these dregs and scum. Hence that immense and diffuse multiplicity of laws which was required in part to overcome discrepancies, and in part to glue together, somehow, the limbs which were severed from their trunk.[26]

The parallel to Hotman is so perfect that we might even charge Bodin with plagiarism did not the date of publication rule this out.[27] And yet another affinity is revealed in Bodin's appeal to universal history. His statement that "in history, indeed, the best part of universal law lies hidden" reads like an echo of Baudouin.[28]

Thus as early as 1559, and most certainly by 1566, Bodin had moved to a universalist position. And along with Hotman and Baudouin he looks to the materials of history for a reformation of juristic science. With Bodin, however, the

[25] *Methodus, Oeuvres philosophiques*, p. 107B.
[26] *Ibid.*, p. 108A.
[27] On the dates of composition and publication of the *Antitribonianus,* see above, p. 36, n. 2.
[28] *Methodus, Oeuvres philosophiques*, p. 109B.

program of reconstruction is not only conceived more theoretically, but in large degree is carried out. Bodin's goal is not *ad hoc* selection of materials as practical requirements suggest, nor general reflections upon history as a supplement to legal education, but a systematic appraisal of law and legislation through a comparison and synthesis of all juridical experience. The only way, he says, "to arrange the laws and govern the state . . . is to collect all the laws of all or the most famous commonwealths, to compare them and derive the best variety." [29] With Bodin, moreover, this enormous project is not handed over to the future but is taken as a present obligation. "To this objective," he informs his patron, "I have devoted all my studies, all my thoughts." [30] Thus the juridical program of Bodin is the first attempt to derive a general theory of law from the materials of universal history. And it involves, as we shall now attempt to show, three methodological departures of profound importance for the future: an exposition of *jus gentium* in the sense of a common law of nations, a system of comparative jurisprudence, and a sociological theory of legal history.

The first and oldest element in Bodin's system, the exposition of *jus gentium*, is a determination of the necessary or most workable principles of law from the uniformities of legal history, that is, from a study of the laws, which all or the great majority of peoples have in common. In the *Juris universi distributio*, which is a study in juristic classification, the phase preliminary to his ultimate procedure is the formulation of a scheme of topics on which every nation has specific rules. "Having omitted," says Bodin, "the classification of the civil law, as the distribution of a single individual, we will go to the *jus gentium* or *jus commune*

[29] *Ibid.*, p. 107B.   [30] *Ibid.*

for the art [or scheme] which we are seeking." [31] As a
result of his reflections on experience and history, he has
come to the conclusion that

> every people, or certainly the better part of peoples, have a
> public law, a private law, legislation by princes, edicts of
> magistrates, laws of sovereignty, various customs and institu-
> tions, and, where law does not exist or even custom, at least
> the principle of equity. They also have some rules of reward
> and punishment, conventions, obligations, testaments, judg-
> ments, decrees, actions of the law, as well as other arrange-
> ments of this sort which conserve the society of man with man
> and which can be included in an art [of law].[32]

Systematically arranged and subdivided, therefore, such
elements common to all systems are the "forms" or
"topics" of *jus gentium*. And around each of these the laws
of all of the most famous peoples are to be systematically
collected and compared in order to display their common
precepts.

The completion of this scheme in all its parts was obviously beyond the powers of a lifetime. But in one area of
great importance the entire program was actually fulfilled.
The central core of the *Six Books of the Commonwealth*
is a systematic exposition, by historical comparisons, of
the various powers of command which in all or the majority of systems are established or recognized in law. In the
Juris universi distributio these basic forms of power, or
the constitutional structure of a social hierarchy, had already been identified and classified. And one of Bodin's
objectives in the later work is to elaborate on each of them
in turn.

All power to command another is either public or private
[he asserts]. The public power resides in the sovereign who
makes the law, or in the person of magistrates who bend

---

[31] *Juris universi distributio, Oeuvres philosophiques*, p. 72B.
[32] *Ibid.*, pp. 72B–73A.

beneath his law and command other magistrates or private persons. The private power to command is in the heads of households, or in guilds and corporations generally. The command of households is grasped in four varieties, the power of husbands over wives, of fathers over children, of owners over slaves, and of masters over servants. And inasmuch as the right government of the commonwealth as a whole, and of corporations and guilds, associations and households, depends on a right comprehension of commanding and obeying, we will speak in order of the power to command, following the scheme that we have posed.[33]

The actual method of this exposition is an elaborate synthesis of legal history which, on one occasion, is described as follows. "At the beginning," says Bodin, apparently referring to the *Juris universi distributio,*

I sketched a form of universal law in outline. . . . Next I laid down postulates on which the entire discipline may rest as on the firmest of foundations. Then I added definitions, and finally precepts known as rules which I set down as briefly as I could according to the outline taken as a norm. On the one side I briefly noted the interpreters of Roman Law so that others may take from the same sources what they wish. On the other side I have appended the laws, universally collected, of all the peoples who have been famous for military and civil training. For this purpose I have used historians as well as jurisconsults so that to the laws of the Persians, Greeks, and Egyptians no less consideration should be given than to the Roman. I have resolved, moreover, to take all the best things from the pandects of the Hebrews also, and especially from the books of the Sanhedrin, in which enterprise J. Cinquarbres and Mercier, royal teachers of the Hebrew language, have promised to assist me. Nor do I doubt that I can arrange to have the laws of the Spanish and the British made available, as well as those of all the more famous cities of Italy and

---

[33] *Six livres de la république,* Bk. I, ch. III, p. 19. The elaboration of this statement constitutes almost all of Bks. I and III, which are the central theoretical portions of the work. The statement itself reproduces, almost verbatim, the definition and distribution of *imperium* in the *Juris universi distributio,* p. 78A.

Germany (for it would be infinite to seek the more obscure) in order to conjoin these with our own. And this too I hope, that we may soon have access to the civil law of Turkey, or that the public law at least, on which this flourishing and formidable power is established, should in one way or another come into our possession. To these, the doctrine of the courts is to be added and the supreme authority of decisions in your court [the Parlement of Paris] and the court of the Empire. . . . All these materials, tested and confirmed by the opinions of jurisconsults and historians, will therefore serve to make this discipline [of law] more brilliant and majestic than if it depended on the judgment of the Roman people only.[34]

Ambitious as it seems, however, this announcement of 1566 is not completely representative of what is actually achieved in the *Six Books of the Commonwealth*. The range of sources, ten years later, is even more expansive and elaborate. In addition to the laws of antiquity, Biblical and classical, of Turkey and western Europe generally, there is now important and original research in the laws of Scandinavia and Poland, as well as some materials, at least, on eastern Europe, Muscovy, North Africa, and America.[35] The search for these materials, moreover, involved not only an exhaustive study of the existing stock of histories, ethno-geographies, and travelers' reports, but wherever possible an intensive consultation of the archives, which was highly productive, one might note, for the legal history of France.[36] And there was also an endless interrogation, both at home and on his trips abroad, of ambassadors, travelers, and foreign scholars which, although it provides

---

[34] *Methodus*, pp. 107B–108A.

[35] On the truly extraordinary range of Bodin's research in general, more precise details may be found in Jean Moreau-Reibel, *Jean Bodin*, *passim* and especially Part I, ch. IV, Part II, chs. III, IV.

[36] One example is Bodin's collection of coronation oaths in Bk. I, ch. VIII, of the *Six livres de la république*.

materials for all of Europe, is especially important for his information on England, Scandinavia, Poland, and Venice.[37]

In the *Six Books of the Commonwealth*, furthermore, the comparative procedure is even more synthetic and constructive. According to the earlier conception, the postulates and precepts arrived at by historical reflection were apparently to be stated in complete abstraction, and the materials from which they were derived were to appear only as appendices or footnotes. But in the final form the definitions and the precepts, for the most part, are constructed step by step through a genuine comparison of laws which are often discussed in considerable detail. The laws of different peoples, furthermore, are related not only to each other but also, in frequent historical digressions, to their background and their circumstances. The penalty, of course, is a certain loss of brevity and order, so that the line of thought is sometimes lost in the details. The gain, however, is an enrichment and deepening of legal insights by a constant process of including and distinguishing materials.

The outcome, therefore, in this part of Bodin's work, is a systematic and exhaustive exposition of the *jus gentium*, or fundamental law, in the area of public power. Moreover, although the method is primarily empirical, this program of Bodin forms a transition to the *jus naturae* of the coming century. In Grotius, for instance, the fundamental law of reason is still associated, more or less, with the common conventions of "the better part of peoples," and there is a heavy dependence upon history, upon examples and opinions from the past, to confirm its several propositions.[38]

[37] See Moreau-Reibel, *Jean Bodin*, Part I, ch. IV. The investigations carried out on Bodin's trip to England are indicated in *ibid.*, Part II, ch. III, pp. 199 ff.

[38] "In order to prove the existence of this law of nature, I have, furthermore, availed myself of the testimony of philosophers, historians,

Grotius, indeed, often relies upon Bodin directly. And in the Prolegomena to *De jure belli ac pacis* the *Six Books of the Commonwealth,* as well as certain monographs of Hotman, are acknowledged as invaluable sources because they combine the study of the law with history.[39]

The second part of Bodin's system is a discrimination of the basic differences in constitutions in order to compare them and determine which is best. Bodin's procedure here can hardly be discussed apart from the substance of his scheme, but the central problem, very briefly indicated, is a reclassification of the forms of polity around his relatively new conception of the commonwealth as a sovereign power absolute and indivisible.[40] On this basis, the ancient forms of rule—democracy, aristocracy, and monarchy—are redefined, in precise and formal terms, as the different numerical principles by which the juristic person of a sovereign is instituted as a single or collective individual.[41]

---

poets, finally also of orators. Not that confidence is to be reposed in them without discrimination. . . . But when many at different times, and in different places, affirm the same thing as certain, that ought to be referred to a universal cause; and this cause . . . must be either a correct conclusion drawn from the principles of nature, or common consent. The former points to the law of nature; the latter, to the law of nations." Hugo Grotius, *De jure belli ac pacis libri tres,* trans. by Francis W. Kelsey *et al.* (Oxford, 1925), II, 23–24. See also p. 26: "History in relation to our subject is useful in two ways; it supplies both illustrations and judgments. . . . And judgments are not to be slighted, especially when they are in agreement with one another; for by such statements the existence of the law of nature, as we have said, is in a measure proved, and by no other means, in fact, is it possible to establish the law of nations." The poets and orators, conversely, "do not have so great weight."

[39] "The French have tried rather to introduce history into their study of laws. Among them Bodin and Hotman have obtained a great name, the former by an extensive treatise, the latter by separate questions; their statements and lines of reasoning will frequently supply us with material in searching out the truth." Grotius, *De jure belli ac pacis,* p. 29.

[40] *Six livres de la république,* Bk. II, ch. I, pp. 251–52.

[41] Here, and in what follows, I do not propose any detailed explanation of Bodin's political and social concepts or any critical comments on their value, since I am interested only in his method.

These, moreover, are held to be the only "states of commonwealth" or forms by which a sovereign is instituted, since a mixed constitution or divided sovereignty is assumed to be politically absurd. On the other hand, the balancing of different social interests, which is what the "mixed constitution" really meant, is now explained by a distinction between the form of government and the form of state. The form of government, or the political principle by which offices and honors are distributed, may be either democratic, aristocratic, or monarchical, or some combination of these three; it need not be in correspondence with the form of state and, indeed, some contrast between the two is recommended by Bodin as a help to political stability. Thus the classical commonwealth of Rome was democratic in its sovereignty, but aristocratic in its government, while the "mixed" constitution of contemporary Venice is really a pure aristocracy with certain democratic tendencies in government.[42] It seems apparent to Bodin, however, that the most harmonious balancing of interests is most readily achieved in commonwealths whose sovereign is monarchic, since the ruler stands above the different classes and may arrange his government more freely.[43]

With these distinctions, therefore, we have the first systematic attempt to rework the classifications of antiquity, and of Aristotle and Polybius especially, into a scheme consistently related to the national sovereignties developing in Europe. In this respect, moreover, there is an

[42] "We have shown before that the state of a commonwealth and its government are different things; for the state may be popular, and the government aristocratic, as was the case in Rome after the expulsion of the kings. . . ." *Six livres de la république*, Bk. VI, ch. VI, p. 1047. See also Bk. II, ch. II, p. 272, where this distinction is called "a secret of policy on which no one has ever touched." On the states of Rome and Venice see Bk. II, ch. I, pp. 257–62, and on their forms of government Bk. VI, ch. VI, pp. 1047–48.

[43] *Ibid.*, Bk. VI, ch. VI, pp. 1048 ff.

attempt to reveal the constitutional character of the European system by an elaborate comparison of "despotic" and "legitimate" monarchies (or commonwealths).[44] The last of Bodin's main distinctions is between commonwealths like those of the Tartars, Muscovites, and Turks, or of the ancient Egyptians, Persians, and Assyrians, wherein the power of the ruler over subjects is like that of an owner over slaves, and commonwealths like those of Europe where the liberty and property of subjects are protected by the rule of law.

But from the standpoint of juristic method, perhaps the most far-reaching innovation is the process of comparison itself. The essential differences in polities, and especially in forms of state, are so universally and copiously illustrated that literally every system known in any way is considered in the light of Bodin's scheme, and classified according to his principles. Under the "aristocratic state," [45] for instance, there is a concise presentation of all available data as to the size, composition, and status of the ruling organs for Pharsalia, Sparta, Epidaurus, Thebes, Rhodes, Genoa, Geneva, Zurich, Basel, Berne, Lucerne, Fribourg, Venice, Rhagusa, Lucca, the German Empire, and finally the political system of Nuremburg considered as representative of Augsburg, Worms, and other independent German cities. Along with this, moreover, the advantages and disadvantages of the different types of constitutional arrangements, and of the forms

---

[44] *Ibid.*, Bk. II, chs. II, III. The distinction, although naturally suggested, as in Aristotle, by varieties of monarchy, is actually a distinction in the types of commonwealth as such, i.e., in the extent of power and not in the form of its ownership. Bodin, indeed, applies the terms "legitimate" and "despotic" to other forms of state as well, although he is vague as to what is meant by a "despotic" aristocracy or democracy. See Bk. II, ch. VI, p. 312, and Bk. IV, ch. I, p. 506. But in any case, despotism, properly defined, is not to be confused with tyranny. The former is a proper form of rule so long as power is justly exercised, while the latter is misrule as such and not considered as a constitutional "form" of commonwealth or state.

[45] *Six livres de la république*, Bk. II, ch. VI.

of state especially, are weighed as systematically as possible with a mass of historical examples the scope of which is almost as extensive. The outcome, therefore, is a comprehensive system of comparative constitutional law, which is a major step in the beginning not only of this special branch, but of comparative jurisprudence generally.[46]

The final part of Bodin's program is a classification of those essential peculiarities of character or polity to which a nation's laws must be accommodated. The types of character, or *naturels*, of people are systematically derived from the influence of climate or geography, in a highly elaborated version of certain notions suggested by the ancients.[47] And since the effects of natural environment are moral as well as physiological, they shape every area of human culture, including legal institutions. Among other things, for instance, the nations of the north and of the mountains have an inclination towards extreme democracy or very weakened forms of monarchy because their natures are sensuous and reckless.[48] The southern peoples, on the other hand, are drawn to theocratic absolutism by their intellectual and contemplative natures, while nations of the middle climes and regions, as in the case of the Romans and the French, have a special capacity for government by law since their natures are moderate and prudent.[49] This nature of a people is not completely determining, to be

[46] Although the history of comparative jurisprudence has not yet been studied in detail, both Sir Frederick Pollock, in his early essay of 1903, "The History of Comparative Jurisprudence," *Essays in the Law* (London, 1922), and also Walther Hug, "The History of Comparative Law," *Harvard Law Review*, XLV, 1027, find the beginnings in the sixteenth century. The work of Bodin and its far-reaching significance, although mentioned by neither of these writers, is the central theme of Moreau-Reibel, *Jean Bodin*. And Bodin is taken as the patron of the study of comparative legal history by the Franco-Belgian Societé Jean Bodin pour l'Histoire Comparative des Institutions.

[47] *Method for the Easy Comprehension of Histories*, ch. V, and *Six Books of the Commonwealth*, Bk. V, ch. I.

[48] *Six livres de la république*, Bk. V, ch. I, pp. 691–93.

[49] *Ibid.*, Bk. V, ch. I, pp. 686–87.

sure, since its effects may be controlled by "training." [50]
But it is a persistent bias, nonetheless, which the statesman
must inevitably consider even when attempting to correct
it, and to this extent, accordingly, it is a fundamental test
of legislation.

It is necessary [says Bodin] that the wise governor of a people
should fully understand its humor and its nature before ex-
pecting anything from an alteration of the state or of the laws.
For one of the most important and perhaps the principal
foundation of commonwealths is the adaptation of the state
to the nature of the citizens, and the edicts and ordinances to
the nature of the places, the persons, and the times. [51]

This relativistic test of legislation, furthermore, is not
restricted to character alone, for although the relationships
are not systematically worked out, the laws and institutions of a people, Bodin indicates, must be adapted to their
form of state. "When commonwealths contrast," he says,
"as do monarchical and democratic states, contrasting
ordinances and laws must be established in consideration of
the [form of] state." [52] And in discussing particular principles of policy such as the length of tenure for the magistrates, or the distribution of rewards and punishments, or
the organization of an army, he frequently attempts to
show the kinds of arrangements which are peculiar to each
form of state or are especially adapted to control their in-
conveniences. [53]

The final aspect of the program, therefore, is a sociological theory of legal differences which is a clear anticipation of Montesquieu's historical empiricism. It may be
noted, also, that in Bodin's system the *naturels* of peoples

---

[50] *Ibid.*, Bk. V, ch. I, pp. 695–96. See also *Methodus*, pp. 164A–B.
[51] *Six livres de la république*, Bk. V, ch. I, p. 664.
[52] *Ibid.*, Bk. II, ch. I, p. 253.
[53] *Ibid.*, Bk. IV, ch. IV, p. 591; Bk. V, ch. IV, pp. 727–30; Bk. V, ch.
V, pp. 747 ff.

tend to be distributed in time as well as space. There has been, he thinks, a constant expansion of the human race, promoted mainly by the growth of population, from an original situs in the fertile south and east to the less inviting regions of the north and west.[54] And corresponding to the changes of climate thus encountered, this expansion in the course of time is marked by a successive differentiation of nations, states, and cultures into a *respublica mundana* or world commonwealth.[55] Thus, in embryo at least, Bodin's theory of legal differences goes hand in hand with a naturalistic philosophy of historical development which broadly anticipates standpoints of the later eighteenth century.

Considered as a whole, accordingly, this historical program of Bodin is the moment of transition, in juristic method, from the exegesis of authority to a universal basis of critical reflection. After four centuries or more of exegesis the system of the medieval Romanist had been destroyed by historical research. And after some sixty years of philological corrections, and of logical reworkings of the whole, it was finally felt that the legislation of Justinian was incomplete and historically particular. The outcome, therefore, is a reconstruction of the art of law on a base of universal history which is of first importance for the history of jurisprudence. For in Bodin's system of comparison and synthesis we have a new set of methodological foundations by which the modern development is influenced—and not only in juristic science but in related social disciplines as well.

[54] *Methodus*, pp. 154B–155A, 242B–243A; *Six livres de la république*, Bk. V, ch. I, pp. 669–71.
[55] *Six livres de la république*, Bk. V, ch. I, pp. 688–89.

PART II

HISTORY
THE BEGINNING OF
A THEORY OF CRITICISM

V

THE EMERGENCE OF
AN ART OF READING HISTORY

The juristic revolution, which has been described in the preceding chapters, is closely connected to the beginnings, in the sixteenth century, of a methodology of historical criticism. In speaking of beginnings we do not suggest, of course, that the sixteenth century is in any sense the dawn of critical awareness in history. A great many critical procedures were already known from the works of ancient and Renaissance historians. And in many of these writings there are comments by the author on his sources or polemics against other writers, in which particular procedures are discussed *ad hoc*. What did not as yet exist, however, was a methodology or general theory of criticism in the developed sense of a system of procedures and techniques focused on the central problem of historical belief. In other words, it had not as yet been specifically and deliberately asked whether, in view of all that is known about the habits of historians, it is ever possible to believe reports about the past, and if so, under what conditions and with what degree of certainty.

In the sixteenth century, however, systematic reflections of this order were promoted by the growing interest of educators in the technique of teaching history to students.[1]

[1] For earlier reflections on history, limited mainly to problems of narrative style and technique, see below, p. 85, n. 4, and pp. 86–87.

The contemporary interest in history has already been illustrated by the program of the universal jurists. For in one
respect their idea of a comparative synthesis of "civil wisdom" was the most comprehensive and profound expression
of the conviction, common in their age, that the universal
study of historians is the ideal mode of acquiring political
and moral prudence. The grounds of this esteem, of course,
were not particularly new, since praise of the lessons to be
learned from reading history is frequently encountered
among the ancients and the early humanists. But in the later
Renaissance the commitment to this enterprise was new in
the degree of its intensity. Political and social thought was
now more heavily oriented towards historical examples and
comparisons than in any period of classical antiquity. And
whereas the ancients had never generally assumed that the
study of the past as such should have equal weight with
philosophy or rhetoric in the curriculum of education, in
the sixteenth century a systematic study of the entire realm
of history was all but universally regarded as a fundamental
goal of education.

But with this new importance attributed to history, a
method of historical instruction, or "art of reading histories" with profit, began to be considered an urgent need.
Very early anticipations of this need are to be found in the
work of Juan Luis Vives whose influential treatise *On the
Teaching of the Disciplines* (1531) contains a section on
the reading of historians in the form of pedagogical suggestions to prospective students.[2] A list of authors is provided
which catalogues all the extant authors of the narrative tradition. And along with this there is advice, chronological

[2] *Opera omnia*, VI, 386–401. The *De tradendis disciplinis* was originally published together with the *De causis corruptarum artium* and the
De vita et moribus eruditi as part of a general treatise, *De disciplinis.*
See F. Kuypers, "Vives in seiner Pädagogik," *Neue Jahrbücher für Philologie und Pädagogik*, CLVI (1897), p. 14.

and otherwise, on the most convenient order for taking up these authors, as well as scattered comments on their usefulness as sources. Thus the idea, embryonically at least, is a method of historical instruction.

But it is not until the time of the universal jurists that such a method is explicitly developed. To Baudouin, we have seen, the very meaning of a more universalist approach was a reform of legal education by an expansion of the old curriculum to include the study of universal history. And as a teacher of the law he actually attempted such a course, his experience with which is undoubtedly reflected in his *Prolegomenon on the Teaching of Universal History and Its Conjunction with Jurisprudence*. In any event, the initial half of this oration is a plea for the reading of historians, along with extended and important comments as to method. Bodin had already moved from the conjunction of history and jurisprudence to an actual attempt at synthesis which was intended to serve a twofold purpose. It was to be not only a comparison and synthesis of laws, but also a set of principles and categories by which the things of greatest value in a history, instances of prudence both in thought and deed, might be properly interpreted and gathered. Indeed, the central ideas of the *Six Books of the Commonwealth* were originally presented as one among a number of suggestions for the culling of "flowers" from the past.[3] And these suggestions, collected as a handbook for the student, are his *Method for the Easy Comprehension of Histories* which established a new genre of historical reflection to be developed throughout the eighteenth century.[4]

[3] *Methodus*, p. 107A.

[4] See below, pp. 153–54. The distinction between these newer arts of reading and the older arts of writing has not been generally noted in the modern literature, in part, perhaps, because the interests of each sometimes overlap. But awareness of the difference may be found among contemporaries. That Baudouin goes off in a "new direction" is explicitly

By the very nature of their program, therefore, the universal jurists, Baudouin and Bodin, make extremely important attempts to constitute an art of reading histories.[5] And from the standpoint thus adopted they are confronted with a set of problems which had never been considered systematically. Systematic reflection on the art of history as it was developed in the ancient world and continued by the early humanists,[6] was all but exclusively concerned with the ideal canons of a "true narration"—with such literary problems,

---

recognized by Antonio Possevino, *Apparatus ad omnium gentium historiam*, pp. 8, 95. Bodin himself, *Methodus, Oeuvres philosophiques*, p. 114A, points out that his work on the method of history is a departure from the works of those "who compose books on writing history, when there is a whole host of books filled with all information on the past, and the libraries are filled with historical works which they might more usefully have proposed to imitate and study than to engage in oratorical disputes on exordia, narrations, and the ornaments of words and sentences." But he is obscure as to the nature of the change. Ernst Bernheim, *Lehrbuch der historischen Methode und der Geschichtsphilosophie*, p. 220, recognizes that Bodin's purpose is an art of "general historical cultivation," but he does not comment on the newness or significance of the genre.

[5] In this brief sketch of the emergence of an art of reading history, I have not discussed the Protestant-Humanist world-chroniclers of Germany. The Christian, and especially Protestant, emphasis on a study of the providence of God in time generally contributes to the interest in universal history which is characteristic of the age as a whole. But early chroniclers like Johann Carion, or Melanchthon, who revised his work, have no special interest in method. Their only contribution is an "order of study" consisting of a formulation and defense of the prophetic schema of the Four Monarchies, a scheme, indeed, which the French humanists are concerned to refute.

[6] The classical, as well as the main Renaissance, sources of this tradition, are provided in an influential collection by Johann Wolf, *Artis historicae penus* (Basel, 1579). A fine survey of the themes reflected in the humanist writings is Beatrice Reynolds, "Shifting Currents in Historical Criticism," *Journal of the History of Ideas*, XIV (no. 4, Oct. 1953), 471–92. The sources of the tradition as a whole are summarized chronologically in Enrico Maffei, *Trattati dell'arte storica dal rinascimento fino al secolo XVII*. For this tradition in relation to Bodin see John L. Brown, *The Methodus of Jean Bodin*, ch. III, and for a general survey of methodological directions in this period as a whole see Friedrich von Bezold, "Zur Entstehungsgeschichte der historischen Methodik," in *Aus Mittelalter und Renaissance*.

therefore, as the proprieties of style and order, the most
edifying kind of topics, and the responsibilities of taste and
honesty in rendering a moral judgment. On all these points
there are important contributions to a rhetoric of history,
which may be referred to as an "art of writing"; and the
various portraits of the ideal writer, critically derived from
classic models, may sometimes be suggestive, indirectly, of
guides to the study of the past. The crucial point, however,
is that problems on the use of documents, considered as a
source of information, are never explicitly confronted since
the very standpoint rules them out. The prospective writer,
to be sure, is occasionally admonished to be diligent in
gathering his facts. But with the one exception of Polybius,
and a few isolated comments elsewhere, the actual labor of
research is considered merely as a stage of preparation and
not as an ingredient of art itself, which is the proper focus
of discussion. Even in Polybius, moveover, the attack on
hearsay evidence, and the insistence on immediate experience or the interrogation of a living witness, are in no way
intended, or developed, as a criterion for using documents.
It is, on the contrary, a prescription directed to the writer,
who is thus explicitly admonished to avoid relying on documents, and to choose contemporary subjects for which such
sources seem of less importance.[7]

But with the perspective of the sixteenth century the
neglected problem is explicitly identified and becomes, indeed, a major issue. Alongside the older arts of writing,
which are continued by the theorists of rhetoric, there is
now an interest in "reading," or an art of studying the past.
In this new perspective the works of individual historians,
including documents of all varieties, are considered not as
literary models but as sources. And the question inevitably
arises as to the general conditions for belief in what they

[7] See below, p. 130, n. 45.

say, the response to which is a methodology of historical criticism.

On this question the findings of Baudouin and Bodin are not completely independent, for the interest in historical criticism is endemic in the sixteenth century and appears in other quarters also. Thus their formulation of the issue in its broadest terms is a response, in part, to a Pyrrhonist attack on reading history from which they have also borrowed certain critical techniques. And their ideas on the philosophic basis of belief are directly paralleled, and indirectly influenced perhaps, by the efforts of a Catholic theologian to justify the use of history in the proof of theological hypotheses. Our present purpose, therefore, is to bring together all these contributions as the components of a common product in which, for the first time, a methodology of historical criticism definitely appears.

VI

THE CHALLENGE OF
HISTORICAL PYRRHONISM

Logically as well as temporally, the first reflections on historical belief were from the skeptical and skepticizing movements which were a pervasive current of the later Renaissance. In their critique of knowledge it was a typical objective of the skeptics to show of all existing disciplines that their basic premises were doubtful and uncertain. And since the reading of historians was increasingly regarded as a special study, it began to be taken as a separate target and its characteristic assumptions specifically attacked. The ground of these attacks, of course, was not some reasoned principle of evidence, but a sophistic and dogmatic negativity. Yet, even so, the reflections of the skeptics played an initial role of great importance in the emergence of a theory of criticism. In attempting to undermine the study of historians, they developed a number of critical conceptions which were taken over by the methodologists. And even more significant, historically at least, is the Pyrrhonist conclusion proper, that historical knowledge is impossible. For it was as an attempt to answer this negation that the theoretical foundations of belief were first elaborated.

In Cornelius Agrippa, who was the first to make extensive criticisms, the skeptical attack on history is pseudo-empirical in form, since it is an attempt to demonstrate,

from a massive "illustration" of the vices of historians, that
the norms of honesty have rarely been observed, and that
the reading of historians is profitless because all, or almost
all, of them are liars.[1] It is, for instance, a widespread vice
among historians to be negligent or credulous in seeking information. And this initial vice may appear in a variety of
forms. Some historians have simply retailed hearsay as the
truth. Others have "observed" but only seen by halves, like
mendicants wandering in pilgrimage. And still others had
no public records and were simply indulging in their own
conjectures.[2] The first corruption, furthermore, affects almost all the geographers of classical antiquity—such as
Eratosthenes, Metrodorus, Speptius, Posidonius, and Patrocles, who are so indicted by their colleague, Strabo. Examples of the second include the reports of Onesicritus and
Aristobulus on India.[3] And the third is illustrated by a

[1] Agrippa was born at Cologne in 1486 and died at Grenoble in 1535.
The work in question is *De incertitudine et vanitate scientiarum* (Paris,
1531), translated as *The Vanity of Arts and Sciences* (London and
Westminster, 1676). Satirical in tone, it was intended, says Agrippa, "to
be a bold and almost Herculean attempt to wage War against the Giant-
like opposition of all the Arts and Sciences." Agrippa's predecessor in
this enterprise is the more scholarly Gianfrancesco Pico della Mirandola
(nephew of the more famous Giovanni), whose *Examen vanitatis doctrinae gentium, et veritatis Christianae disciplinae* was first published in
1520. If Pico has rather little to say about history it is most likely because his skepticism, for the most part, follows Sextus Empiricus very
closely.

In Juan Luis Vives, *De causis corruptarum artium*, which appears in
Opera omnia (Valencia, 1782), and was originally published in 1531,
there is a similar illustration of vices in historians which is quasi-skeptical
in tone. Except for comparative purposes, I do not discuss it here, since
it does not come to any Pyrrhonist conclusion.

[2] *The Vanity of Arts and Sciences*, pp. 27–28, 32.

[3] "For the most of Historians, because they were not living at the
same time, or were not present at the Actions, or conversant with the
Persons, taking their relations upon trust at second hand, mist the chief
scope of Truth and Certainty. Of which Vice Eratosthenes, Metrodorus,
Speptius, Posidonius, and Patrocles the Geographer, are accused by
Strabo. Others there are, who having seen by halves, as in a March, or
as Mendicant Travellers to perform Vows, viewing many Provinces,

famous passage from Josephus in which the entire tribe of Greek historians is implicated—not only Hesiod, Hellanicus, and Agesilaus, who were poets and logographers, but historians like Herodotus, Ephorus, and Timaeus.[4] "This," Agrippa adds maliciously, "Josephus writes of others whom notwithstanding our Hegesippus very severely corrects." [5] But if so many and so "reputable" reporters have either had no sources or were careless, what reason to believe that others have not done the same? And if these and maybe all historians have pretended to know what they did not, how then erase the doubt that they have lied in other ways as well?

Such doubts are further strengthened by an even more glaring aspect of mendacity, the vice of deliberate invention, which is also multiple in form. Some historians have written "For the Fables sake" and "feign" upon the truth of history either by twisting truth to fit the fable or converting everything to fiction.[6] The examples here are not only Herodotus and certain medieval authors, but even Romans like Trebellian and Tacitus [7]—the first accused by

---

undertake to compile Histories; such as formerly Onesicritus and Aristobulus set forth concerning India." *Ibid.*, pp. 27–28.

[4] The passage in question is from Josephus' polemic against Apion and is widely quoted in this period. The disagreements and mutual recriminations of the Greek historians are cited by Josephus as "confirmation" of his basic charge against their whole historiography, that they neither have nor keep sufficient public archives. "Nay, who is there that cannot easily gather from the Greek writers themselves, that they knew but little on good foundation when they set about writing, but rather jotted down their own conjectures as to facts?" And the "principal cause" of this is "the fact that from the beginning the Greeks were careless about public records." Translated in James T. Shotwell, *The History of History*, pp. 155–56.

[5] Agrippa, *Vanity of Arts and Sciences, p.* 32.   [6] *Ibid.*, pp. 28–29.

[7] The charge against the Greek historians as frivolous and "poetic" is suggested by comments and asides in Roman critics, which the Renaissance takes over wholesale, and especially so since these charges seem supported by Josephus who has almost canonical authority. Thus Vives, *De causis corruptarum artium, Opera,* VI, pp. 103–4, and also Melchior

Flavius Vopiscus and the second by no less authorities than Tertullian and Orosius. Other writers are too proud to admit that they are ignorant, or to show that they have borrowed from another, or to appear anything less than universally informed, so that almost all geographers are full of figments like "Troglodytes" and "Pigmies" which the gullible accept as oracles because labeled with the title "History." And others still are so taken with their own philosophy that they presume to tell a noble lie and "do not relate how things were done but how they ought to have been done." [8] Of this genre are not only the ideal portraits of the medievals but the figure of Cyrus in Xenophon.[9]

But the worst and most contemptible historians are those "deserving double blame, who though they were present at the transactions themselves, or otherwise knowing the carriage and management of things, yet overcome by favor or affection, in flattery of their own Party, against the Faith of History, will confirm Falsity for Truth, and deliver to Posterity a wrong accompt of things." [10] And to this, the most ubiquitous and sovereign of vices, the paths of temptation seem peculiarly numerous. Some have written out of fear and hatred. Others, including Orosius, a church historian, have sought only to justify an action and have written history like legal briefs.[11] Others still, like almost all the

---

Cano, *De locis theologicis* (Bassani, 1776; original edition Salamanca, 1563), XI, vi, p. 240, as well as Bodin, *Methodus*, p. 124A. Agrippa simply extends this to the Romans also.

[8] Agrippa, *Vanity of Arts and Sciences*, p. 31.

[9] This criticism, like that of Herodotus for being not the "father of history but the father of lies," is also endlessly repeated in this period. It should be pointed out that these, like most critical judgments on the ancients, are taken second hand from ancient critics.

[10] Agrippa, *Vanity of Arts and Sciences*, p. 29.

[11] Agrippa, however, is very cautious on "writers of the church." But his contemporary, Vives, is much bolder: "Nor is there any greater care for truth in writing of the acts of saints. . . . Each one of these [authors] wrote their acts as his affections moved him, so that it was bias and not truth which wrote the history. How unworthy of God and Christian

Greek historians,[12] Sabellicus, Paulus Aemilius, Gaguinus, have desired only to extol their countrymen and vilify the deeds of others.[13] And yet others, including all the German

men that history of the saints which is called the *Legenda aurea!* Why they call it 'golden' I cannot understand, since it was written by a man of iron tongue, and leaden heart! What, indeed, could be more disgusting than this book? Oh, what a shame it is to Christians, that the most excellent acts of our saints have not been recorded more truthfully and more accurately—whether for the purpose of knowledge or for the imitation of such virtue—when the Greek and Roman authors wrote with so much care of their leaders, philosophers, and sages!" *De causis corruptarum artium, Opera,* VI, 108.

What Vives and his contemporaries fail to appreciate, however, is that writings of this sort, especially in the early middle ages, were often the result of sheer naïveté rather than mendacity. A charming example of this attitude is reported by G. G. Coulton. "Somewhere about A.D. 850 Agnellus, Bishop of Ravenna, undertook to write a complete series of lives of his predecessors in that see. He was, for his own time, a remarkable scholar; yet here is his description of his historical methods. 'Where I have not found any history of these bishops, and have not been able by conversation with aged men, or inspection of the monuments, or from any other authentic source, to obtain information concerning them, in such a case, in order that there might not be a break in the series, I have composed the life myself, with the help of God and the prayers of the brethren.' " *Medieval Panorama,* p. 439.

[12] Once again the "chauvinism" of the Greeks is a universal complaint uncritically borrowed from the Romans, and based on an exaggeration of the "virtue" of the latter. Cf. the following attack in Vives: "But this boastfulness of Greeks about themselves, became even greater and more impudent after the greatness of the Roman people began to obscure the glory of the Greeks. . . . Plutarch [for example] wrote a massive work *On the Lives of Famous Greeks and Romans in Comparison* and another, somewhat briefer, *On the Similarity of Greek and Roman Actions* which he entitled *Parallels.* To begin with, what unfair comparisons. Does Rome produce a Marcus Cato or a Claudius Marcellus, the Greek opposed an Aristides or Pelopidas; does Rome bring forward Brutus, the Greek produces Dio. It is a match between Mirmillions and Thracians. And what labor there is in the arrangement, what anxiety on the part of this learned and not ineloquent man to display the pairs of likes and unlikes as though they were of equal magnitudes! How like a shoemaker does he chew until the hide is stretched! Indeed, if there are places in the *Parallels* which he has undertaken to supply, and cannot do so from the facts, he simply fills them on his own, so that shameful voids and gaps will not offend his reader or slight the reputation of the Greeks." *De causis corruptarum artium, Opera,* pp. 106–7.

[13] The main targets here are the first products of the early humanist school of historiography. Leonardo Bruni, Poggio, and Polydore Vergil

chroniclers, to say nothing of the ancients, are inventors of fantastic genealogies to glorify a people or a prince.[14]

In the history of history, accordingly, every kind of lying has repeatedly occurred, and in the "illustration" of these vices almost every writer has been implicated. Nor does it matter to Agrippa that his indictments are often second hand and that some may therefore be unfounded. In almost every case they have been leveled by historians themselves so that either the accused or the accuser is a liar, and very often both. And it is the assumption of the skeptic, furthermore, that where two opinions contradict there can be no basis for belief in either.[15]

But by a similar procedure the doubt about historians may be even further reenforced by citing cases of dissentience

---

might also have been mentioned. The aim of these was to create, for each of the states and cities of the moderns, a "national epic" of their civic virtue directly modeled on the style of Livy and even, sometimes, on his content. In the later period the revulsion against these is general. See again Vives, *ibid.*, p. 107, for an early statement: "In transmitting actions of more recent memory, the Frenchmen write of France; the Italians of Italy; the Spaniards of Spain; the Germans of Germany; the English of England, and others likewise, for the sake of some specific nation. The author of these things thinks that the only charge which he has undertaken is to inflate that people as much as he is able, and does not turn his eye to truth but to the reputation of that nation. This, they think, is how a history is written: to emphasize, dilate, embellish, and extol if that nation has done anything outstanding; and if it has acted ignominiously or basely, to conceal, to elevate, to extenuate, to defend, and to excuse. These fools do not consider that this is not to write a history, but to plead that people's cause, which is for a patron not for an historian."

14 The reference here is to the rash of genealogies, often medieval in their origin, which were worked up by the humanists of northern Europe to provide their peoples with an ancestry as old and as illustrious as that of the Italians. Bodin, *Methodus*, IX, devotes an entire chapter to refuting some of these, especially the German, which were most notorious. Bodin's "corrections," however, are often as absurd as the errors they replace.

15 It is this element of dissentience which helps to explain the special pleasure that Agrippa takes in the passage from Josephus mentioned above, p. 91, n. 4.

in testimony. For if two narrations of the past conflict it is a possibility at least that one, or both, of the historians has either invented or knowingly repeated lies. And if they disagree on facts which both could check the probability is all the more enhanced. The showing of dissentience, therefore, as the aspect of a whole tradition or as a feature of "history" in general is a means of raising wholesale doubt. Thus Gianfrancesco Pico della Mirandola already uses it to cast a shadow on the "faith" of pagans whose variant traditions on the origins of Rome are pointedly contrasted to the marvelous concord of the Bible.[16] And it is taken over and extended by Agrippa as a final assault on the whole fraternity of historians. "For historians," he says, "are at such variance among Themselves, delivering several Tales of one and the same Story, that it is impossible but that most of them must be the greatest lyers in the World. For to omit the beginnings of the World, the Universal Deluge, the Building of Rome, or of any other great City, from whence they generally commence the first beginnings of their Huge Narratives—of which they are all altogether ignorant, of the other generally very incredulous, and of the third very uncertain what to determine. For these things being the most remote in time, more easily gain Pardon for Vulgar Error. But as to what concerns later times and ages, within the memory of our Ancestors, there is no excuse that can be admitted for their Lying." [17] The apparent

[16] As to the founding of Rome, "many of the Latins are in conflict with many of the Greeks; there is variation of the Greeks among themselves; nor are all the Latins in agreement with each other. Some would have it that Rome was founded by the comrades of Aeneas, and named for Romus, Aeneas' son; others that it was somehow founded by Aeneas, and named Roma for a Trojan woman; in the preference of others the city and its name will derive from Romus, son of Circe and Ulysses; in others from Evander; and in others yet from others still." *Examen vanitatis doctrinae gentium et veritatis Christianae disciplinae* in *Opera omnia Ioannis Francisci Pici Mirandulae*, p. 915.

[17] Agrippa, *Vanity of Arts and Sciences*, p. 27.

"pardon" on the distant past is not, of course, a real concession, but merely a sarcastic preterition.

The principle of doubt, accordingly, is that there have been so many kinds of lying, so many cases of mendacity, and so many dissentient traditions that there can be no basis for historical belief. As against the proposition that historians have wished to tell the truth it may be argued, with equal plausibility, that all or most historians "are the greatest lyers in the world." And since the historian who lies about one thing may just as well have lied about others, the Pyrrhonistic conclusion that nothing in history is certain seems well founded. Or, as Agrippa dogmatically expresses it, "there is no exact truth to be found in Historie, though it be the thing we most seek for there." [18]

From a finite number of defections and discrepancies it is thus inferred that the ideal of a historian never was nor ever will be realized. In Agrippa, therefore, the Pyrrhonistic basis is "empirical." But by 1560, with the work of Francesco Patrizzi, the skepticizing neo-Platonist, a theoretical dimension is supplied.[19] The question now is not how many historians have lied, and how often, but whether

[18] *Ibid.*, p. 32.

[19] Francesco Patrizzi (1529–97) is more a neo-Platonist than a skeptic. But it should be noted that the skepticizing of the sixteenth century, the doubt of human knowledge, is very frequently associated with neo-Platonism, Christian fideism, or both. See Agrippa, *Vanity of Arts and Sciences*, Allocution to the Reader, and Pico, *Examen vanitatis*, p. 913. Historical Pyrrhonism, furthermore, may be held independently of Pyrrhonism generally since history is not a form of theoretic-intuitive knowing. In any case the fifth of Patrizzi's *Della historia diece dialoghi* (Venice, 1560) is a major contribution to historical Pyrrhonism. This element is completely neglected in the only study of these dialogues, by Franz Lamprecht, *Zur Theorie der humanistische Geschichtsschreibung, Mensch und Geschichte bei Francesco Patrizzi*. There is, however, a brief discussion of this dialogue in E. Maffei, *Trattati dell'arte storica*, pp. 47–50.

I have used the Latin version of Patrizzi's work included in *Artis historicae penus*, ed. J. Wolf (2d ed., Basel, 1579).

a "good historian" is possible at all. And the denial is thoroughly ingenious.

The historian, begins Patrizzi, was either contemporary with the action or was not. And in the latter case his veracity is hardly worth discussing. He may or may not have distorted what he learned. But even granting his integrity he is clearly dependent on the truthfulness of others. For whether the past be "recent or remote," "there is nothing that can be known of it but what our forbears have transmitted through their writings."[20] In the first distinction, therefore, that between original and secondary authors, the issue of historical veracity is narrowed to the prime observer.

But this original observer, notes Patrizzi, will either be a party to the action or a neutral. And in the former case he will have the strongest motives to distort. He will either vilify his enemies from hatred, glorify his party from affection, keep silent on his hidden interests, or perhaps do all of these together. The partisan observer, therefore, is so very likely to have lied that everything depends upon the neutral.

The difficulty here, however, is that a neutral reporter is not very likely to be knowledgeable. Unattached to either party, he will not have been privy to their counsels and must depend on what the actors tell him. These, however, are not very likely to reveal themselves to neutrals, as is especially clear in the behavior of the prince who is in possession of the secrets of the state. The prudent ruler, holds Patrizzi, is a natural enemy to truth since the basis of his power is in cunning while his authority depends on reputation. If he communicates his secrets, it is normally to confidants and servants, who have every motive to preserve

[20] Francesco Patrizzi, *De historia dialogi X*, in *Artis historicae penus*, I, 457.

them in affection, interest, or fear.[21] It is very likely, therefore, that the "honest neutral," even granting his existence,
will know only the outcome of an action and not the inner
motivations on which the value of a history depends.[22]

Yet another alternative, however, is found in works of
history which have been written from the "public annals"
—like the pontifical annals of the Romans, the Persian annals
of Megasthenes the Greek, or those of Berosus the Chaldean which had recently been "rediscovered." These, concedes Patrizzi, were unbiased. But public annals, he objects,
have the same limitation as the "neutral." They contain
"nothing but the outcome of events and perhaps a mention
of the time, but very little on the other things which are
necessarily expressed in histories . . . the actors, the occasions, the place, the time, the modes and instruments of action—for all these things are requisite if something is to be
accomplished." [23] But in supplying these details the historian is likely to invent. And hence "from true annals a false
history . . . is readily concocted." [24]

Suppose, however, that all historians agree about a point.
Even here, Patrizzi argues, there can be no presumption of

[21] " 'Is it, then, surprising,' he went on, 'if princes, the shrewdest
among men, should wish their deeds to be admired either for binding
their subjects to themselves, or for overawing others?' 'Not at all,' I
said, 'but how do they accomplish this?' 'By hiding their vices and their
counsels,' he replied, 'and by displaying their power and their riches.'
'True enough, but how is this an obstacle to truth in history?' 'Because
they wish,' he answered, 'that historians pass over their vices and inepti-
tudes, and make no mention, even, of the strategy by which they have
succeeded, unless perhaps it be some kind of thing which might add
lustre to their power and authority. . . . And this [the revelation of the
truth] is a thing of even greater difficulty in that princes and leaders
should keep their counsels prudently secret, and not allow them to get
out to anyone unless he be extremely faithful.' " *Ibid.*, pp. 463–64.

[22] "But if, indeed, he be free of hate or friendship, and depend on
neither party, he will be unable to investigate the counsels of the parties
at first hand, which are the most important thing in transactions of this
sort." *Ibid.*, p. 458.

[23] *Ibid.*, p. 465.   [24] *Ibid.*

veracity since the truth is not revealed by those who know it. And so "even of those who nicely correspond, I still should say that they had only written of a thing which was passed around in rumor." [25] Neither annals nor concordance, therefore, is an answer to the main dilemma.

Patrizzi's contribution, then, is to postulate a "good historian," a neutral observer or a follower of annals, and then to demonstrate that he cannot get the vital information. And the method, clearly, is a shrewd and subtle confrontation of the pragmatic norm of history with the pragmatic theory of politics. According to the first, the condition of a useful history is that the observer have the "inside" story.[26] But according to the second, the prime condition

[25] *Ibid.*, p. 466. On this final point Patrizzi has mentioned a procedure, the comparison of testimony, which undermines his thesis that no historical statement is "certain." And his answer is evasive and suspiciously brief. Moreover, in the sixth and succeeding dialogue, which deals with the problems confronting an author of universal history, he includes agreement of testimonies as one of three things which provide a modicum of confidence. "Moreover, in order for anyone to find some path in this confusion [of the sources], there are three things to be observed which may bring some light to the reader: the consensus of chronologies; events described by a variety of different authors in the same way; and the location of regions of the globe. By all these things the truth of history is grasped." *Ibid.*, pp. 469–70. I do not think, however, that Patrizzi is insincere or is simply trifling in Dialogue V. In the first place he remains essentially skeptical in Dialogue VI. Here too he constantly laments that exactitude is not to be expected. And if he recommends comparing sources it is not as a means of gaining certainty on crucial points of "action," but only, as the context indicates, to determine the broader outlines of events, a possibility which he admits, as we shall see, in Dialogue V. In the second place, there seems to be no author of the sixteenth century who has any clear notion of the comparison of *contemporary* sources. And it is probable that Patrizzi did not really recognize the value of a procedure which was not fully formulated until much later.

[26] This is clearly implicit in Polybius' principle of "autopsy" which was well known to the later Renaissance. (See the digressions in the *Histories* generally, and especially the polemic against Timaeus in Book XII.) Polybius, however, is unaware that the insistence on eyewitness history, at least as he conceives it, is a condemnation not only of the use of other people's works as sources, but also of his own!

of a prudent actor is to keep his secrets to himself.[27] The terms of a "truthful and instructive" narrative are thus exposed as incompatible. The historian may either be impartial or informed. But he cannot be both at once. And since this dilemma is "original" no remedy can possibly exist.

It is this incompatibility, finally, which underlies Patrizzi's "consolation." The human story, he concedes, is "truthful," but only *grosso modo*—in its coarser outlines—which means that it is "uninstructive." [28] Or, if one prefers another consolation, an untrue "history" may still be full of useful lessons, and need only be reputed truthful to have all its pedagogical effect—which means, of course, that it is no longer "history" at all.[29] The entire notion of pragmatic history is thus ironically turned against itself. It can be either precise in illustrating lessons or generally true. But it cannot be "exactly true." And it is in this ironic sense that Patrizzi comes to the conclusion of Agrippa. "It is utterly

[27] Patrizzi's remarks on princes and leaders are obviously borrowed from the "Machiavellian" school of Italian political thought.

[28] "Is there not, then, some remedy for this disease of history, or some kind of consolation for us, I said? This one consolation is remaining to us, and that is to believe that the course of history extending from the beginning of the world to our times is truthful in the coarser sort of way, and especially that the outcomes of events, in many cases though not all, are written as they actually occurred. But the things narrated of counsels, tactics, and other aspects of affairs can never be entirely true." Patrizzi, *De historia dialogi X, Artis historicae penus*, I, 458–59.

[29] "If you wish, Contilis, that I tell what came into my mind concerning this, I should say that it is a matter of indifference whether history be true or false . . . because it suffices that the opinion (*fama*) should exist that things have happened in this fashion or the other. . . . I have been asking of Borghesius . . . whether he would not agree, as to the goal of history, that from its examples the attainment of felicity is learned more clearly . . . [and] I know that Vergil wished that men should learn the attainment of felicity through his poetry. . . . No doubt, he said, but what then follows? That it makes no difference whether history be true or false since we can learn felicity from fables and inventions. . . . [But] there can be no history [he answered] except of true occurrences. . . ." *Ibid.*, pp. 459–60.

and totally impossible," he says, "for human actions to be known as they were actually done." [30]

These attacks upon belief in history are a new achievement in the history of skepticism which is not surpassed until the nineteenth century.[31] But they are of even greater moment for the theory of history, as an initial, if exaggerated, statement of certain fundamental principles of criticism. The most important, surely, is that all historians are subject to an element of doubt, that it cannot be presumed, in other words, that their statements are "exactly true." In the vices mentioned by Agrippa we have a primitive listing of the forms of historical distortion. And Patrizzi's finding that the plans and motives of an action are the class of subjects on which truthfulness is least to be presumed is not only ingenious but substantially correct.[32]

[30] *Ibid.*, p. 458. It may be noted that this conclusion, constantly repeated, as well as the "defense" of history, is an indirect attack on Patrizzi's teacher, Francesco Robortello. In opposition to Giovanni Pontano who held, in accordance with Quintilian (*Institutio oratoria, liber decimus*, I, 31), that "history is poetry written without meter" (*Artis historicae penus*, I, 545), Robortello, expanding on a point in Aristotle (*Poetics*, 9), argued that history is "the narration of things done as they were actually done" (*Artis historicae penus*, I, 893). Patrizzi's break with this perhaps explains the pathetic tone of the dialogue. Patrizzi constantly takes Robortello's position and is just as constantly defeated. It is true, however, that there is no disagreement between pupil and teacher as to what history ought to be.

[31] The ancient skeptics were generally indifferent to history either because the theoretical issue was less inviting than in "nomothetic" disciplines, or, more likely, because the "reading of historians" was less developed as a cultural activity. In any event, Sextus Empiricus, who is the main source for the revival of Pyrrhonism, makes only a passing reference to the "fact" that all historians are liars in the course of his attack upon grammarians (*Against the Professors*, I, 266–68). The next phase of historical Pyrrhonism is to argue that the truth about events is *unknowable*, not only to posterity, but even to observers and participants. But this requires a conception of the relativity of historical judgments which does not really develop until the nineteenth century.

[32] "It is easy to see why the remoteness of the scholar from the object of his knowledge makes so strong an impression on many historical

Throughout his argument, moreover, there are shrewd reflections on the characteristic limits of the different types
of sources.

The limitation of the skeptics, on the other hand, is their
illegitimate demand for certainty, by which doubt is turned
into an absolute. And as a result of this their conclusions
are outrageously exaggerated—as in the leap from the finding of error in an author to the presumption of complete
mendacity, from the mendacity of some to that of all, from
secrecy in certain situations to the silence of everyone on
everything, and, worst of all, from the "inexactitude" of
history to the inference of total uselessness. The critical
findings of the skeptics, therefore, are drowned in a dogmatic negativity. To this extent they remain the tactics of
lampoon or irony and are not as yet a theory of criticism.

---

theorists. It is because they think of history primarily in terms of events,
even of episodes—of a history which, rightly or wrongly (and it is im-
material at the moment) attaches an extreme importance to the exact
reconstruction of the actions, words, or attitudes of a few personages,
brought together for a relatively brief scene, in which, as in a classic
tragedy, are marshaled all the forces of the critical moment: the day of
a revolution, a battle, or a diplomatic interview." Marc Bloch, *The Historian's Craft*, pp. 50–51. Patrizzi, of course, sees only the negative aspect
of this point, and not its positive aspect, the relatively greater value of
institutional research. Here too, however, the scientific view does not
develop fully until the later eighteenth or the nineteenth century.

VII

MELCHIOR CANO
THE FOUNDATIONS OF
HISTORICAL BELIEF

The first constructive contributions to the problem of historical belief make their appearance in the 1560s with the
work of Melchior Cano, the Dominican theologian of the
school of Salamanca, and the jurist-historians, Baudouin
and Bodin. With Cano, whose ideas are slightly earlier, the
problem arises from a methodological movement in Catholicism for which his treatise *De locis theologicis* (On
the sources of theology) is regarded as the classic formulation.[1] A theological method, in the present sense, is the

[1] Cano (1509–60) was a student of Vitoria to whose chair at Salamanca he ultimately succeeded. He was an imperial nominee to the
Council of Trent (1551–52) and bishop of the Canaries (1552–53). As
an inveterate opponent of the Jesuits and a nationalist he became involved in serious difficulties with the papacy towards the end of his life.
On the work of Cano, generally, and on his crucial importance for the
theological method of modern Catholicism see Albert Lang, *Die Loci
Theologici des Melchior Cano und die Methode des dogmatischen
Beweises*, in *Münchener Studien zur historischen Theologie*, Vol. VI,
from which the preceding biographical sketch is derived (pp. 1–8). See
also M. Jacquin, "Melchior Cano et la théologie moderne," *Revue des
sciences philosophiques et théologiques*, IX, 121–41, and two articles in
the *Dictionnaire de théologie catholique*, "Lieux Théologiques," by A.
Gardeil who, along with Lang, is the outstanding commentator on Cano,
and "Théologie" by M-J. Congar.
  Cano's treatise was composed between 1543 and 1560, and according
to Lang the last two books, in the first of which history is treated, were

proof of theological hypotheses by a demonstration of their
positive authority. But in the sixteenth century the traditional system of authorities, normally unquestioned in the
middle ages, had been explicitly rejected by the Protestants.
And within Catholicism Erasmus and the humanists had attacked the school theology for ignoring or misusing sources
in its passion for casuistic speculation. From both the apologetic and the reformist standpoints, therefore, the need
existed in the Counter Reformation for a definition of the
sources of belief, and of the grounds and degree of their
authority—which is what is meant by a "dogmatic methodology" or, as it is sometimes called, a "fundamental" and
"positive" theology.[2] Tendencies in this direction are already to be found in the early polemics against Luther, in
some of the decrees laid down at Trent, and in the reforms
of pedagogic method introduced at Salamanca by Vitoria.[3]

---

composed after 1553. Cano's work therefore is earlier than Patrizzi's,
Baudouin's, and Bodin's. And since it was published posthumously at
Salamanca in 1563, it could not have been known to Baudouin. Whether
Bodin made use of it is extremely difficult to determine.

[2] *Dogmatic* methodology" in that the proof of propositions depends
not on the rationale of their content but on the authority from which
they are derived, and "methodological" in that the basis and ranking of
these authorities is systematized. Hence it is a "positive" approach to the
proof of "theological conclusions." And at the same time it is a "fundamental" theology in that it attempts to define, within the scope of faith,
the sources from which faith has been derived. It can thus be understood
why the work of Cano is regarded by historians of Catholic theology,
if not as a negation of the method of St. Thomas, at least as a whole
new branch of theological science decisive for the modern viewpoint.
Alongside "speculative theology," it is "positive dogmatics." And hence
the work of Cano, says Lang, "rightly deserves to be taken as the beginning of modern theology." *Die Loci Theologici des Melchior Cano*,
p. 6. See also Jacquin, "Melchior Cano et la théologie moderne," *Revue
des sciences philosophiques et théologiques*, IX (1920), 121–41.

[3] On the methodological element in early polemicists against Luther
such as Cochlaeus, Fisher, and Pighius as well as in the decrees of Trent,
see Pontien Polman, *L'Élément historique dans la controverse religieuse
du XVIe siècle*, pp. 284 ff.; and also Lang, *Die Loci Theologici des
Melchior Cano*, pp. 43–45. Among Vitoria's reforms were a greater
emphasis on sources and a more humanistic style (which becomes truly

But it is not until the *De locis theologicis* of Cano that they
are developed in a systematic fashion.

The purpose of this work, as we have said, is a system
of authorities. Hence Cano's notion of a *locus* or a "place"
is radically different from traditional usage. In Aristotle
or Cicero a "topic," "place," or "head of argument" is
either an argument or a class of arguments considered useful in debate or oratory. And schemes of places in this
sense, such as those of Ramus or Agricola, are highly regarded in the Renaissance, where they are known as "methods of invention," or "arts" of "finding" arguments. These
general schemes, however, were normally used in order to
collate arguments related to each other by their content, as
in the *Loci communes* of Melanchthon which groups related principles of Protestant theology. In Cano, on the
other hand, the place or *locus* is the source from which an
argument is taken and to which it is referred for proof of
its dogmatic status. And his enterprise, accordingly, is not
to be confused with a Catholic version of Melanchthon's.
Cano's purpose is not to give a scheme of contents, but to
identify and justify the various sources by which theological propositions are dogmatically confirmed, and to evalu-
ate their relative authority.[4] The evaluation of authority,
moreover, is a highly complicated problem since the pro-

elegant with Cano). It is, in some respects, a theological counterpart to
the humanist movement in jurisprudence, but not as radical, of course,
since the authority of St. Thomas is not only recognized but now de-
finitively established. On Vitoria, see Lang, pp. 51–52.

[4] Cano's classification of places was influenced by Agricola and Cano
sometimes refers to his own work as a "method of invention," which, in
a rather special sense, of course, it is. On Cano's reworking of the concept of *locus*, and the application of this concept in dogmatic methodology, see Lang, *Die Loci Theologici des Melchior Cano*, pp. 55 ff.
There is also a more technical discussion in Gardeil, "Lieux théologiques," in *Dictionnaire de théologie catholique*, IX, 713–47, who tries
to create a system of his own from Cano's.

bative value of a source will often vary in degree according to the type of argument for which it is invoked.

Of the ten sources identified by Cano some are proper and the rest extrinsic. The sources proper to theology are those whose truths are more or less inspired—the Scriptures and the "Oral Gospel";[5] the infallible decisions of the Church—as a totality,[6] in council, or in the Church of Rome as represented by the pope; and, under certain circumstances, the opinions of the Fathers and of the Scholastic Doctors. The extrinsic sources, on the other hand, are the sciences in general, philosophy, and history, whose truths, although founded only upon reason, are essential to theology as a means of clarifying faith.

The admission of this latter class is not, of course, a new idea, for it is explicitly defended by St. Thomas and is obviously required by that total unity of faith and reason on which Thomistic theology perennially insists.[7] What is significantly new, however, is the way in which the subdivisions of this category reflect the scientific preoccupations of the age. In St. Thomas the truths of human reason are all lumped together in "science" or "philosophy." In Cano, on the other hand, philosophy and history are separated, and the special problems of the latter are identified. This special interest in history is the result, quite obviously, both of his positivistic standpoint towards theology and his extensive culture as a humanist. With the shift of emphasis from dialectical expansion of the principles of faith to an intensive study of their sources, the appeal to history, in disputation as in exegesis, becomes a fundamental mode of

[5] Essential to Catholicism as a means of explaining apparent gaps between its doctrine and the Scriptures. See Polman, *L'Élément historique dans la controverse religieuse*, pp. 303 ff.

[6] I.e., the common opinion or practice of the "entire" Church considered in a sense similar to customary law.

[7] *Summa theologica*, Part One, Quest. I, Art. 8, Reply Obj. 2.

argument.[8] And it is Cano's conclusion as a humanist that "there are many things which history supplies us from her treasuries, which if we lack, whether in theology or in almost any other discipline, we will be very often found arid and unlearned." [9]

History, therefore, is treated as a separate source, and the question, for this as for all the other *loci*, is to determine under what conditions and with what degree of certainty an argument derived from it is probative. It is at this juncture, and in this fashion, that Cano's problem in dogmatic methodology demands a systematic inquiry into the foundations of historical belief, an inquiry, indeed, the novelty of which he seems to recognize. "What must be established first," says Cano, "is the nature and degree of human history's authority, and how much faith theology may place in it, a question which up to now has never been decided. And next, what kind of author should be considered probable and trustworthy, which is the thing most difficult of all. For since in theological disputes the explication of the truth must often be extracted, not from the recent speech of men, but from the ancestral memory and ancient annals, it is necessary, and on ancient history especially, to be of sober judgment, to be thoroughly familiar with all of the historians, and to discriminate the truthful from the false." [10]

The first part of Cano's inquiry, epistemological in nature, is at once a definition of the logical basis of historical belief and a running answer to contemporary skepticism. Historical belief, as Cano recognizes, the belief, that is, in

---

[8] These uses of history were traditional, of course. New, however, is the emphasis on this procedure and the sense of its distinctive value, as in the statement, for example, that "there are many places in the Holy Scripture which cannot be decided without a cognizance of human history." *De locis theologicis*, p. 204.

[9] *Ibid.*, p. 203.   [10] *Ibid.*, p. 205.

the existence of a past event, is initially grounded in the good faith of the person who reported it. And it requires, therefore, a certain modicum of faith in human goodness which is precisely what the skeptic would refuse. But it is obvious enough, says Cano, that some belief in human nature is essential to humane existence. Civilization would collapse without it, since it is by the faith of pupils in their teachers that any art or science is transmitted, including the very principles of speech. And society itself would perish, since human relationships depend on trust.[11] The answer, therefore, essentially borrowed from St. Augustine,[12] is that the inclination to believe in others is a moral and practical necessity.[13] And from this it follows that the dogmatic skeptic, who completely refuses to believe, not only declares himself an enemy of mankind, but involves himself in latent contradiction. By his very behavior as a social being he shows that he is willing to believe and thereby acts against his principle.[14]

But although it effectively reveals the absurdity of skepticism, this Augustinian justification of belief is only an opposing dogmatism unless the conditions and the limits are

[11] *Ibid.*, p. 208.

[12] Cano cites him as his main authority. The key sources are *On the Utility of Believing* and *On Faith in Things Unseen.*

[13] "From which it comes about, that the author of nature impressed a natural inclination to believe upon the minds of men; and indeed faith is as necessary for the life and education of a man, as is the highest place to fire, and the lowest to earth in order that they properly exist." *Cano, De locis theologicis*, p. 208.

[14] The polemical point is sharper in Augustine: "I will not mention how much those, who rebuke us for believing what we do not see, themselves believe of rumor, or history, or about places where they themselves have never been; nor how in those instances they do not say: 'We do not believe because we have not seen.' Because, if they say this, they are compelled to admit that they are uncertain about their own parents. For, even on this point they have believed by the reports of others. . . ." *On Faith in Things Unseen*, in *Fathers of the Church: Writings of Saint Augustine*, II, 453.

supplied. And it is the specification of these elements, as applied to the evidence of history, which is Cano's most important contribution.[15] He recognizes, to begin with, that "apart from sacred authors . . . there is no historian who has not lied on something." [16] And he is thus in agreement with the skeptic that the statements of a single author can never be taken as a certainty. But at the same time there is a class of "serious" historians—of which "some undoubtedly exist"—who have generally wished to tell the truth, and are only rarely deceitful or deceived.[17] Since their statements, therefore, are more likely to be true than false, the authority of such historians is the basis for a probable belief.[18] And this is understood by Cano as a kind

[15] St. Augustine, to be sure, frequently indicates that there is a difference between belief and credulity, and that the former has its limits. But he is not at all concerned to specify these limits and to explain the difference, for example, between probable belief and faith, for his very purpose is to justify the latter as being not unreasonable by giving common illustrations of the former. "Therefore, when we do not believe what we cannot see, concord will perish and human society itself will not stand firm. How much more, then, ought faith to be placed in divine things, even if they are not seen. If this faith is not applied, it is not the friendship of some men which is violated, but the very essence of religion itself, so that the very depth of misery results." *Ibid.*, pp. 455–56. History, moreover, is merely one such illustration in which one believes on "faith" as in the loyalty of a friend.

With Cano, on the other hand, the major focus is on history, a form of limited belief, and the central problem is therefore to define conditions.

[16] Cano, *De locis theologicis*, p. 208. The idea that no historian can help but err is from a passage in Flavius Vopiscus. And since the word "lie" appears in it, it is widely cited in the sixteenth century, especially by skeptics. Thus Gianfrancesco Pico della Mirandola, *Examen vanitatis*, p. 915.

[17] On this point, the "statistical" absurdity of the skeptic innuendo that all historians are "simply" liars, the classic statement is Bodin's: "It is not very likely that among so great a multitude of writers not one is to be found who is led to writing by neither entreaty, nor bribe, nor envy, nor emotion." *Methodus*, p. 124B.

[18] "Serious and trustworthy historians, of which sort some undoubtedly exist both in ecclesiastical and secular affairs, provide the theologian with a probable argument either for corroborating propositions of his own, or for refuting false opinions of his adversaries." Cano, *De locis theologicis*, p. 208.

of moderated skepticism halfway between credulity and doubt. In the reading of a serious historian "both are justly reprehended: the person who believes too quickly, and the one who is too slow in his belief." [19]

A probable belief, moreover, is subject to a reasonable doubt, which is distinguished from dogmatic doubt by the specific nature of its grounds and target. It is, on the one hand, the very essence of the skeptic's insolence to reject the attestation of a good authority without reasons either relevant or probable, without, that is, a specific showing, based on independent evidence, that the statement doubted is intrinsically implausible.[20] And it is yet another aspect of this same mistake, when isolated statements of an author have been rejected on specific grounds, to assume that the doubt may be indefinitely extended. "For if we should conclude," says Cano, "that some things reported by Pliny or other very serious historians, being scarcely credible, did not occur, we do not, by that alone, destroy the history's authority." [21] Cano's meaning, therefore, is that for any statement a probable basis of belief exists when two independent factors come together—a determination that its author is generally credible, and a finding of intrinsic plausibility. "For there is no one," he concludes, "of good education and properly disposed towards human life who will not believe a serious man reporting something which is credible." [22]

From this premise Cano goes on to make his final point that "If all [of a great number of] tested and serious historians concur about the same event the argument drawn

[19] *Ibid.*, p. 209.

[20] "But there are a number of people in this age of ours who perversely, not to say imprudently, cast doubt on things which have been attested by very serious historians. If these were to give relevant and probable reasons they should perhaps be listened to. But since they give none they are to be despised. . . ." *Ibid.*, p. 209.

[21] *Ibid.*, pp. 208–9.   [22] *Ibid.*, p. 208.

from their authority is certain." [23] Without qualification,
to be sure, this conclusion is too simple. Thus in counting
his authorities Cano draws no distinction between original
and secondary sources or, with respect to contemporary
testimony, between independent and derivative accounts.
Nor does he consider here or elsewhere the related question of conflicting testimony.[24] Moreover, there is no situation in which a historical report is really "certain." But
within these limits we have a satisfactory view of the probative value of reenforcing testimony and its relationship
to probability. In Cano's previous discussion of reasonable
doubt he has already suggested that even stronger grounds
of doubt are needed where the fact in question is in "the
mouths of two or three." [25] And he is now concluding that
where a great number unanimously agree no argument at
all is possible—as in the unanimously attested fact that
Peter made his seat at Rome. The underlying ground,
however, is even better indicated by the supporting geographical analogies. "What could be sillier," he asks ". . .
than to say that the kinds of monsters, which are spawned
in the Red and Indian seas, do not exist because we never
saw the like? . . . It would be as if the Mediterranean peo-

[23] *Ibid.*, p. 209.

[24] On the last two points there is passing comment in Bodin. There is,
first, a warning that in cases of supporting statements "one historian
may be misled by the error of another." And this is the apparent
ground of his opinion that the case for certainty is greatest when
authors in agreement on a point are in conflict on related aspects. There
is, second, a recognition by Bodin that statements on a point may be
conflicting. And his suggestion here is to pursue the more "probable"
or "necessary" version, which will most often be the latest, he believes,
since the truth emerges slowly as bias disappears. (On these points see
Methodus, pp. 126B, 127A.) It cannot really be said, however, that
Bodin's comments reflect any new theoretical development. For although
his perspective is generally similar to that of Cano and Baudouin on the
problem of historical belief, except for these passing comments he makes
no effort to expound his views at length. His main concern, as we shall
see, is with the critique of particular historians.

[25] Cano, *De locis theologicis*, p. 209.

ples were to deny the existence of the ocean, or if those who were born upon an island in which they saw nothing but little hares and foxes should not believe in the lion and the panther, or if, indeed, we should mock at him who speaks of elephants." [26] In each of these examples, a report which might seem absurd to one of limited experience is nonetheless "sufficiently" attested. The principle, accordingly, which is explicitly noted at one point in Bodin, is that even where a statement is improbable, the inclination to withhold belief may be weakened and ultimately overcome by the weight of accumulated testimonies. "But if a historical report," Bodin remarks, "has so many and so trusted witnesses that it cannot be easily refuted, then even if it seems incredible there is a powerful basis for believing in its truth, and especially so if the authors disagree on its remaining aspects." [27] A historical "certainty," accordingly, is a report attested beyond reasonable doubt.

With these ideas of Cano we have, for the first time, a reasonably correct description of the elementary logic of historical belief. He has understood, with full awareness of the basic implications, that belief in a historical event is a varying degree of probability depending on the value and the number of authorities. And if the formulas have not been fully qualified, and are not as yet developed from a general theory of evidence,[28] his analysis of probability, his empiricist notion of a moderated skepticism, and even his geographical analogies are a clear anticipation, in the sixteenth century, of the more polished argument of Hume.[29]

[26] Ibid.   [27] Methodus, p. 126B.

[28] Although its potential import is universal, the "belief" in history is still restricted, implicitly at least, to the area of "belief in things unseen," or "belief in authority" as opposed to certain demonstration. Hence it is not related, as in Hume, for instance, to an entire empirical epistemology.

[29] Thus Hume on probable authority and reasonable doubt: "The reason why we place any credit in witnesses and historians is not de-

The second part of Cano's inquiry is "whether there be any rules, or 'indices' of history, by which the faith and truth of a historian may be investigated." [30] But on this, the methodological issue in the stricter sense, the progress is relatively slight. Of the three criteria which Cano offers, the first is "integrity and probity," or the inclination of an author to tell only what he saw or heard,[31] and the second is capacity for judgment, or the prudence of an author in selecting and judging his informants when his evidence is secondhand.[32] The third criterion, irrelevant for our purposes, is that no other principle is necessary when the Church has rendered an opinion.[33]

The difficulty, clearly, is that Cano's first two standards are so completely vague and moralistic as to be all but useless as criteria of choice. "Judgment" and "integrity," in other words, are inward dispositions of the mind which cannot be observed directly. From the practical standpoint they are the very things which have to be discovered. And the precise obligation of a critical technique is to infer the

rived from any *connection* which we perceive *a priori* between testimony and reality, but because we are accustomed to find a conformity between them. But when the fact attested is such a one as has seldom fallen under our observation, here is a contest of two opposite experiences, of which the one destroys the other as far as its force goes. . . . " See "Of Miracles," in *An Inquiry Concerning Human Understanding*, pp. 120–21. See also Hume's illustrations which follow this passage.

[30] Cano, *De locis theologicis*, p. 230.

[31] *Ibid.*, p. 238: "The first law is drawn from the integrity and probity of men. And this is thoroughly germane since in narrating something historians attest that they have either seen themselves or have heard from others who have seen."

[32] "The second law, indeed, required in the judgment of a history is that we give preference to those historians who, in addition to a natural austerity, have added a certain prudence in selecting and in judging." *Ibid.*, p. 240. Cano, here, is thinking mainly of the capacity to discern the truth in reports which may be partly suspect.

[33] *Ibid.*, p. 240. This law, although obviously irrelevant from a secular standpoint, is a major problem for Cano, who tries to defend and rationalize all the major pronouncements of the popes and councils on individual church historians.

existence of these qualities from specific indices of conduct, such as the personal background of the author, the characteristics of his style, or his special relation to the subject he is treating. Cano's question, therefore, has, to this extent, been begged. He has promised us a critical procedure by which a good authority may be discriminated. But all he really tells us is that an authority of goodness is required.

Cano himself is marginally aware of this defect. And in his discussion of the first criterion he pauses briefly to propose a remedy. "A writer's integrity and probity," he says, "(for some may ask for this) . . . may sometimes be apparent from his very writings, but is also known from reputation, from the serious and frequent testimony of those who went before us." [34] But these proposals, although promising, are not followed up. Reputation, Cano seems to think, is merely the received tradition, at second-hand or even worse, so that the question still remains as to how the reputation was originally derived. And what he means by a study of the "writing" is a general impression of "crookedness" or "straightness," not the discrimination of specific qualities. [35]

There are one or two other suggestions, finally, which are also worthy of remark. Of somewhat less significance, perhaps, since the notion was generally accepted, is the observation that religious vows are not an automatic guarantee of truth. A pagan, Cano argues, may be naturally inclined to truth, while there are many Christian writers, and even ecclesiastics, who have been shown by Vives to be frequently mendacious. [36] Cano thinks, however, that the best of Christian authors, the Fathers of the Church, for

---

[34] *Ibid.*, p. 240.   [35] *Ibid.*, p. 243.
[36] *Ibid.*, p. 238. This comparison leads Cano to the same enormous sense of shock and indignation as it did Vives, whom he cites.

instance, have a special claim to be believed, and that the task of keeping public annals is most properly the province of a priesthood.[37]

Of much more importance, on the other hand, is a growing awareness of the rules of authenticity. Since an author's character, holds Cano, is the basic guarantee for what he says, it is a prima facie basis for suspicion if he presents himself as other than he is. And he warns the reader that anonymous and pseudonymous works should be rejected, and that very well-known names are sometimes forged.[38] In view of his long discussion, elsewhere in this book, of the most celebrated of contemporary forgeries, these last ideas of Cano are a latent concept, I believe, of the role and basis of "external criticism." But since his general remarks are rather brief I shall explore this problem in another context.[39]

Cano's contribution, therefore, is a clear definition of the problem of historical criticism and a roughly correct formulation of its logical foundations. Both of these are major contributions, and they are presented with a clarity and sense of system which is a refreshing exception to the manner of the age. But on the rules of criticism proper there is a certain poverty and a lack of consequence which are broadly related to his standpoint. Cano's problem as a theologian is not so much the specific ways in which history is criticized, but the most general grounds of its admission as authority.

[37] *Ibid.*, p. 240. This idea of priestly annals is very widespread in the period and derives from a high respect for the priestly annals of the Romans, Chaldeans, Persians, and Egyptians alluded to in classic sources. Cf. Baudouin, *De institutione historiae universae*, p. 131, and more clearly, Bodin, *Methodus*, p. 126B.

[38] Cano, *De locis theologicis*, p. 239.   [39] See below, pp. 121 ff.

VIII

FRANÇOIS BAUDOUIN
THE TYPES OF SOURCES
AND THE TESTS OF AUTHENTICITY

But with Baudouin, and especially with Bodin, a concern with the theory of evidence arises somewhat more directly from the educational problems of a universal history. The universal jurists, we have seen, were drawn to the construction of a course in history, in part as a response to general pedagogical objectives, and in part as a reform of legal education. And in either author an actual method for studying the past, or "art of reading history," becomes the object of a special inquiry.

In Baudouin, this discussion of the reading of historians is closely connected with an apologetic for the enterprise as such. He begins, accordingly, with some arguments for universalism which are among the deepest statements of contemporary attitudes. The first of these is an application of the Christian notion that the providence of God is exhibited not only in nature but in history.[1] The morally instructive, therefore, is not confined to any time or place,

---

[1] "For here [in history], no less than there [in nature], we will be steeped in the sense and wonder of things divine if only we are not too blind and stupid. Indeed, God's concern and action here is even greater." François Baudouin, *De institutione historiae universae et ejus cum jurisprudentia conjunctione prolegomenon*, pp. 8–9. See also pp. 11–12.

for it is the miracle of providence that no matter how de-
based an age may be, there is always some commonwealth
or group in which the persistence of goodness is attested.[2]
Nor are only these examples to be studied, to the exclusion
of the vicious and repulsive, for even "in the gloom of
things the wondrous governance of God shines forth,
which, by human agents doing one thing, contrives to
bring about another which we ought to observe and admire, and almost to adore."[3] In Baudouin, furthermore,
this idea of providence in history is tacitly but clearly separated from the prophetic schema of the four universal
monarchies.[4] And hence the universal study of the past is
not the mere confirmation of a plan already given, but the
revelation of providence itself.[5]

[2] "But there are and have always been kingdoms, commonwealths, or
families in which there was some domicile for letters, humanity, law,
and order; and through all the centuries God had some seat of his kingdom also in this globe, and an attestation of his interest in men." *Ibid.*,
p. 10.

[3] *Ibid.*, p. 23.

[4] The concept of four monarchies—the Babylonian-Assyrian, the Persian, the Greek, and the Roman-German—as the structure of the "world"
or secular domain in the last four of the six millennia of history was
especially appealing to the Protestant humanists of Germany. The old
patristic doctrine, based upon the prophecy of Daniel, was resurrected
and refurbished in Carion, and then taken over and developed by Melanchthon and Sleidan to become the standard German philosophy of
history up until the eighteenth century. The initial attack upon this view
is by the French. And the original and classic answer is the brilliant
seventh chapter of Bodin's *Methodus*, which became a constant issue
among the Germans for a century and more. It might be noted here,
moreover, that just as the French are freed from German parochialism
by their traditional opposition to the empire, they are led to break with
the Italian preoccupation with classical antiquity by their position as
"Northerners" and "Goths." And it is for such reasons, I suspect, that
theirs are the first reflections on the scheme and periods of universal history from a modern standpoint. See, in addition to Bodin, Louis LeRoy,
De la vicissitude ou varieté des choses de l'univers.

[5] "I say that this [the study of history], indeed, is a way and means by
which we may arrive at that understanding of divine and human things
which can place our minds, uplifted, on a height from which we may
observe, as in a mirror, whatever has been done within the world from

But the second and more crucial element is the strictly methodological conception, in part suggested by the ancients, that the particular events of history are a complex of empirical connections which cannot be understood in isolation.[6] One side of this is the organic relationship of social institutions—the interaction of the church and state, of civil and military policy, of one region's affairs upon another.[7] The other, and the more significant side, is the idea of continuity in time—the need, in every case, to trace causes back to the beginning, and consequences forward to the end, for which Baudouin's decisive illustration is the Janus aspect of the fall of Rome.[8] History, therefore, is an empirical totality in space and time—a "universitas" of all

---

its beginning which is worthy of our notice and rememberance. Such priests, indeed, does history produce. . . ." Baudouin, *De institutione historiae universae*, pp. 27–28.

[6] The source constantly used is Polybius, *Histories* I, 4: "And it has always seemed to me that men, who are persuaded that they get a competent view of universal from episodical history, are very much like persons who should see the limbs of some body, which had once been living and beautiful, scattered and remote; and should imagine that to be quite as good as actually beholding the activity and beauty of the living creature itself." This statement is paraphrased very closely by Vives, *De tradendis disciplinis* in *Opera omnia*, V, 393, and is quoted and developed by Bodin, *Methodus*, pp. 116A–116B, and Baudouin, *De institutione historiae universae*, p. 38. But all of these authors, unaware, are using the concept much more broadly than Polybius. For whereas the context of the passage in the latter is the demand for a universal treatment of a history in space, they are thinking mostly of a universal history in time, a concept with which Polybius is not at all concerned.

[7] Baudouin, *ibid.*, pp. 48, 49–51, 70. And see above, p. 44, nn. 24, 26.

[8] "Wondrous, indeed, that stream (Euripus) of human things to be observed in history: the remarkable vicissitudes, incursions, and emigrations of the peoples and the nations, in reciprocating movements as it were. But who sees anything at all in these, who does not see the whole? I believe, indeed, that there are many who prefer to look on Rome triumphant over other peoples rather than the barbarians, conversely, swooping down on her, and devastating Italy in dire vengeance. . . . But from that devastation and such ruins the kingdoms were established which we now admire and in which we live. And their foundations, to whose understanding we cannot be indifferent, cannot otherwise be rightly grasped." *Ibid.*, p. 69. On the theme of continuity, see also pp. 45 ff.

that has occurred, and an "indivisibility in some sense natural." [9] And its parts, to be properly distinguished and related, must be ordered as a single sequence from the beginning of creation to the present.[10]

But although universal history has now been shown desirable, the proof must still be given, says Baudouin, that knowledge of the past is possible. And it is from this apologetic standpoint that he is next confronted with the problem of belief. The records of the past, he would concede, are a "commixtio" of fact and fiction, for "there is scarcely any history on which there is not some fable spattered like a blemish." [11] Therefore it is the obligation of a reader to be cautious. "But there are certain censors," he protests, "too importunate and rash, or should I say morose, who as soon as they note [some error] in a writer, reject the whole of him disdainfully and haughtily, or rip him contumaciously apart. . . ." And "if we should do the same," he asks, "what then will we have left of history?" [12]

The problem, therefore, is a refutation of the Pyrrhonist

[9] *Ibid.*, pp. 47–48. This idea of the "indivisibility" of history, together with the idea of continuity and the divorce of history and nature, is often uncannily suggestive of the historicism of the nineteenth century. And it is perhaps for this reason that Bezold alludes to Baudouin as a "precursor of Mommsen." *Aus Mittelalter und Renaissance*, p. 367. Two important clarifications, however, are required. First, Baudouin's view is more widespread than Bezold seems to realize, for the ideas of the indivisibility of history and of continuity are fully stated in the passages of Vives and Bodin cited above. The concept of a "historical universe" is thus a general contribution of the period. Second, these early views are to be distinguished from those of the nineteenth century on one decisive point. There is no conception yet of any evolutionary process. The standard view, in fact, is an endless series of vicissitudes in history— productive, to be sure, of novelties and regulated in their oscillation by some law or providence, but not necessarily progressive. See Bodin, *Methodus*, ch. VII, and LeRoy, *De la vicissitude*.

[10] "And so, just as it will be inchoate without its true beginning, it is not to be left off until brought to its conclusion." Baudouin, *De institutione historiae universae*, p. 47.

[11] *Ibid.*, p. 73.

[12] *Ibid.*, p. 75. The danger of "excessive" criticism is elaborately illustrated, pp. 76–82.

objection which is here presented in the form of "hyper-criticism." And the epistemological aspect of the answer is roughly parallel to Cano's. "It is one thing," says Baudouin, "to invent deliberately in history, and quite another to add on something sometimes through imprudence." [13] Hence a distinction is elaborately drawn between "myth-historians" who lie intentionally and serious authors who generally wish to tell the truth and in whom the existence of error is an accident. Since the statements of the latter are likely to be true, they may be accepted with an attitude of caution which is halfway between credulity and doubt.[14] And although the guarantee of truth is never perfect, the inclination to believe, with caution, is not only moral according to Augustine, but sanctioned in the law court as a practical necessity.[15]

The various components of this argument are not as systematically connected as with Cano, and no distinction is attempted between the probability and certainty of testimony. But the basic position is essentially the same, and is even more forcefully expressed. "It is the mark," Baudouin says, "of an impudent and fractious man, if something probable is said and has a serious author as its witness, to reject it contumaciously as false, without being able to refute what is affirmed, or to state a reason for rejecting it. As for me, indeed, whenever I read good and serious historians, I am reminded of the old saying: either this must be enough of witnesses, or I do not know what is enough." [16]

[13] *Ibid.*, pp. 73–74.

[14] "Let us always hold on to and remember this, that in the reading of histories we should be of the sort that Aristotle speaks of, who are neither boys, nor yet old men, whose inclination to believe, I say, is neither too easy nor too difficult." *Ibid.*, p. 87. See also p. 84. The variations on this theme are almost endless. Others are to be found in Bodin, *Methodus*, p. 124B.

[15] Baudouin, *De institutione historiae universae*, pp. 88–91.

[16] *Ibid.*, pp. 84–85.

This discussion of the logic of belief, along with constant repetitions of the need for caution, is the main concern of this part of the oration. And the methodological issue in the stricter sense is never deliberately posed. But in the course of the reply to Pyrrhonism there are a number of significant digressions into problems of external criticism, in the sense of rules for identifying authorship. And although some of these are found in Cano, I have chosen to discuss them here because Baudouin's treatment is fuller and more ramified.

In both authors the immediate occasion for reflections of this sort was provided by the celebrated forgeries which had been published by Annius of Viterbo in 1498 and thereafter rapidly exposed.[17] *The Donation of Constantine*, surprisingly, and its exposure by Valla among others, is passed over almost without mention.[18] Among humanists, apparently, whose criteria were mainly literary, it was not especially identified as the forging of a work of "history," and the issue was less narration of the past as such than the present jurisdiction of the Church.[19] The

[17] Originally published as *Antiquitatum variarum volumina XVII cum commentariis.*

[18] Very briefly in Cano, *De locis theologicis*, pp. 207, 228, and in Vives, *De causis corruptarum artium*, *Opera omnia*, VI, 107. In neither case is there reference to Valla. The most surprising fact, however, is that Baudouin does not refer to it in any way, although he is a Protestant and devotes several pages to the corruptions of church history. *De institutione historiae universae*, pp. 100–4.

[19] In Vives, the *Donation* is approached mainly from this legal standpoint. And so also in Cano. The context for Cano is the question of ecclesiastical censorship of history. The reference to the *Donation* appears as the fourteenth objection to the use of history—on the grounds, namely, that although "a history, which has been approved by the supreme pontiffs is supposed to excel all others," the *Donation of Constantine*, accepted by the Church, is false (*De locis theologicis*, p. 207). And his answer (p. 228) is simply an apologetic for the papacy, which never said, holds Cano, that the *Donation* was absolutely true, or that the jurisdiction of the Church primarily depended on it. In Valla the exposure of the forgery is an oratorical attack upon the papacy, on

"finds" of Annius, however, were what Fueter calls a forgery in humanistic style—a creative, and perhaps well-in-
tentioned effort to improve upon a poor tradition in order
to reveal the past.[20] What was presented now was nothing
less than an entire series of annotated texts on the earliest
periods of ancient history.[21] And since most of these were

---

behalf of the king of Naples, for attempting to extend its jurisdiction
by resorting, either ignorantly or deliberately, to a lie. "They [the
popes] say that the city of Rome is theirs; theirs also the kingdom of
Sicily and the kingdom of Naples, as well as the entirety of Italy, and
the lands of the French, the Spanish, the Germans, and the English;
theirs, finally, the entire occident. For all these things are contained in
the pages of the *Donation.* Hence all things are yours, supreme pontiff;
and it is your intention to recoup them all. To despoil the kings and
princes of the West, or to make them pay you yearly tribute, this, indeed, is your design. But I, conversely, think it more justly permitted
to the princes to strip you of all that you obtain through your do-
minion. For I shall show that this *Donation,* whence the supreme pontiffs
would have it that their right was born, was known as little to Sylvester
as to Constantine." *De falso credita et ementita Constantini Donatione
declamatio,* p. 4.

[20] Eduard Fueter, *Geschichte der neueren Historiographie,* p. 135. The
contrast is to medieval forgers whose aims were normally more immediate and practical. "Their fabrications were designed to serve as the foundation of some particular legal claim."

[21] The texts, as well as Annius' learned and bizarre conjectures on
genealogies and etymologies, are a real work of the historical imagination. According to Cano, furthermore, Annius was pleased to think that
he had at last discovered an infallible "criterion" for the judgment of
historians. His texts included the "annals," or rather the historical accounts allegedly derived therefrom, of the Babylonian and Persian monarchies. These, together with the "annals" of the Greek and Roman
empires, were a complete set of the "annals" of the four monarchies.
And since these could surely not be wrong, it had only to be discovered
whether historians agreed with them or not, in order to discriminate the
truthful from the false. "The first rule, he says, is this. All those are to
be accepted without argument who have written in public and attested
faith (*qui publica et probata fide scripserunt*). Second, the acts and
annals of the four monarchies can be rejected or denied by no one, because they were noted down exclusively in public faith, and were preserved in libraries and archives. . . . The third rule is that those who
write only from hearsay or opinion are to be rejected as mere private
persons unless they are not in disagreement with the public attestation.
From which it follows that no one is to be accepted as a chronicler
unless he is in harmony with the annals of the four monarchies." Cano,

"lost" works of historians such as Xenophon, Antoninus Pius, Cato, Fabius Pictor, Philo, and other authors famous in antiquity, they were already intriguing to the humanists. The longest and most precious texts, however, were the annals of Berosus the Chaldean, a writer of the Hellenistic period, whose outline of the race from its beginnings was supplemented by two other finds—the annals of Manethon the Egyptian and the "Persian" annals of Megasthenes the Greek.[22] Contained in these was novel and exciting information on the exotic empires of preclassical antiquity which added to the Biblical accounts. And there were indications of the origins of peoples which were especially welcome to the Northern humanists in their efforts to create, for their respective nations, impressive and "superclassic" genealogies.[23] In each of these historians, moreover, there was some peculiarly attractive basis of authority. All three had based themselves, reputedly, on "annals"; their statements often harmonized with Scripture; Manethon and Berosus had been priests; and the latter had won praises from Josephus. From every standpoint, therefore, they appeared to be fundamental sources.

As already indicated, this balloon was rapidly exploded— first by Raphael Volaterranus and other humanists of Italy,

---

De locis theologicis, p. 230. Annius, it should be noted, claimed to have acquired his texts from two Armenian monks and may have actually believed that his finds were authentic.

[22] All three were Hellenistic writers of the third century B.C.

[23] On these genealogies, see Paul Joachimsen, *Geschichtsauffassung und Geschichtsschreibung in Deutschland unter dem Einfluss des Humanismus*, chs. IV and VI; and Hubert Gillot, *La querelle des anciens et des modernes en France*.
The appeal of Annius' finds to the genealogical imagination may be illustrated by the following passage from his version of Berosus: "There were several Ogyges. The first was the above-mentioned great ancestor of Ninus whom the Babylonians surnamed Gallus because he snatched up and gave life to other survivors in the flood." From this passage Annius goes on to an extended commentary on the names of the Gauls. *Berosi . . . antiquitatum Italiae ac totius orbis libri quinque*, p. 16.

and then, repeatedly, by Beatus Rhenanus, Vives, Cano,
and Baudouin.[24] But even in the third quarter of the century the pseudo-Berosus was still accepted by "many of the
learned."[25] And this persistence, very often, was less a failure to acknowledge the exposure than an inability to see why
a "history" so useful and informative should be given up simply because its author is unknown. This, for example, was
the apparent standpoint of Chytraeus, whose opinion others
must have shared. "I am not unaware," he says, "of the
judgment of Ludovicus Vives and Beatus Rhenanus on
Berosus; nor would I make so bold as to insist that the five
books of antiquities, which are circulated with the commentaries of Annius of Viterbo, are really the work of that

[24] Some of these are very brief. In Cano, however, we have a lengthy
and complete discussion not only of Berosus but of the pseudo-Philo and
pseudo-Magasthenes as part of his attempt to refute Annius' criterion of
history. The "annals" of the monarchies are useless as a test because the
Greeks never had them; those of the Romans were destroyed in large
part, and the annals of the others are no longer extant because Annius'
sources are forgeries. See *De locis theologicis*, pp. 230–38.

[25] Baudouin, *De institutione historiae universae*, p. 81: "But I am
amazed that fragments ascribed to Berosus which a certain monk named
Annius has published in recent years have been able to impose so easily
even upon many of the learned." This, in 1560. And it may be noted
that Francesco Sansevino, a reputable Italian scholar, published an Italian
translation of all the Annian fragments in 1583.

In the interest of justice, however, I should like to correct the hasty
conclusion, of Bezold among others (*Aus Mittelalter und Renaissance*,
p. 381), that Bodin was credulous of the Annian forgeries. This would
seem to follow from his many references to Berosus in his chapters on
chronology and on the origins of peoples. But in the former chapter he
specifically says of Manethon, Megasthenes, and Berosus that "Of these
there remain only scanty fragments, if indeed they were written by
these men." *Methodus*, p. 235A. And in his catalogue of sources which
terminates the work he refers to the "purported" fragments of Manethon
and Berosus. Similarly he mentions Archilochus and Xenophon, p. 236A.
It is clear, therefore, that although Bodin, overwhelmed by his naive
delight in antiquarianism, cannot forbear from citing the forgeries on
occasion, he invariably warns the reader with some such phrase as "si
modo fragmenta illa scripserunt." What he seems to have felt, from a
brief remark on p. 236A, is that he had the "real" Berosus in a corrupted
form. And in one respect, of course, he did, in so far as Annius' version
followed comments on Berosus and his work in Josephus.

Berosus who lived in the time of Alexander, whose Babylonica are cited by Athenaeus . . . and Josephus, and of whom Pliny says . . . there was a statue with a golden tongue at Athens. It is manifest, however, that this little volume of antiquities of Berosus and of Annius is neither disagreeable nor useless to the reader, and that it throws extraordinary light on many places in the Bible, in Diodorus Siculus, and in Dionysius of Halicarnassus as well as other writers. Certainly, the origins and increases of all peoples, and of the very oldest kingdoms, as well as the 38 kings of the first, Assyrian, monarchy continuously presented in a series from Nimrod to Sardanapalus, are extant nowhere else but in Berosus. . . . " [26] The idea, apparently, is that a history is after all a history even if the identity of its author is uncertain.

But as Cano and Baudouin recognize, a principled rejection of the forger is inherent in moderated skepticism, for if lying is admittedly widespread, an unidentified historian is subject to an a priori doubt.[27] Moreover, the very refusal of an author to reveal himself is a specific basis for doubts of his good faith, and especially so if he has traded on another's reputation.[28] And the basic rule of caution, there-

[26] David Chytraeus, *Chronologia historiae Herodoti et Thucydidis recognita, et additis ecclesiae Christi ac imperii romani rebus praecipuis, ab initio mundi usque ad nostram aetatem contexta*, pp. 39–40. A version also appears in Wolf, *Artis historicae penus*, II, under the title, *De lectione historiarum recte instituenda*. Here, too, there is a bare possibility that Chytraeus regards the Annian Berosus as a corrupted version of the real one. But if so he neither makes nor recommends an effort to discriminate the valid element.

[27] Especially clear in Cano, *De locis theologicis*, p. 239: "Greatly suspect are those histories, which indeed bear the name of some particular author, but who or of what sort he is, is uncertain and obscure; of such an order are certain stories put forward not too long ago, of which both the authors and the places were so distant and remote, that whether the first were lying it was impossible to discover, and whether the latter existed it was possible to doubt."

[28] "They [forgeries] have the odor of advantage-seeking men's imposture, or of offspring spawned by heretics, as Gelasius himself points out." *Ibid.*, p. 239.

fore, which is not at all self-evident, is that "we do not in any way embrace those histories which are presented with uncertain signature," [29] and that "we must be diligently on our guard against spurious and counterfeited books on which the name of some great author has been falsely and speciously inscribed." [30]

In both these authors, furthermore, there are exposures of Annius' forgeries in which a critical technique is indicated. Since the false Berosus was an imitation of a partly known original, the method here was to compare the document in question with what is reported of the real one by a good authority. And it is thus established that the pseudo-annals are often contradicted by a summation of Berosus in Josephus, and also that there are things left out which are referred to by Josephus, while others are included which, if authentic, he would probably have mentioned.[31] For the annals of Megasthenes, however, where the original was more obscure, or for a chronology attributed to Philo, where there was no evidence that any had existed, an alternative method was required. The procedure here is to compare the style and contents of the document with the established facts as the author might have treated them. And the authentic mode of treatment is inferred either from the characteristics of his other works, or from the remarks of older authors who had known them. It thus turns out, for instance, that the pseudo-Philo contains mistakes not only on profane but on scriptural events, and shows a certain crudity of style, which can hardly be attributed to a cultivated biblicist and scholar.[32] In general, therefore, the

[29] *Ibid.*
[30] Baudouin, *De institutione historiae universae,* pp. 86–87.
[31] *Ibid.,* p. 82; Cano, *De locis theologicis,* pp. 233–35.
[32] After showing that the *De temporibus* is not mentioned in catalogues of Philo's work in Eusebius, Jerome, and Suidas, as well as establishing a list of errors, Cano goes on to conclude: "Surely the only kind

tests of authorship are criteria of style and content constructed, often with very great sophistication, from the entire range of relevant materials.[33]

In Baudouin, finally, the warning against forgeries is closely connected with two further rules on authenticity. The first of these is a demand for critical editions, since it frequently turns out, he warns, that the cause of a historian's "mendacity" is to be discovered in the errors of his copyists. What he advises, therefore, is the humanist technique of emendation which had been so successfully applied to the textual correction of the *Corpus Juris*.[34] This, however, is regarded as the task of specialists whom the student is expected to consult. And for this reason the technique is not exemplified.

But the second and more elaborate discussion is of even greater interest since it is an approximate but real appreciation of the special value of original materials. The occasion for this argument is an attempt to find further reasons for historical belief in analogies to courtroom practice. And it begins with the important observation that the conditions of the former are less perfect.[35] In court, Baudouin points

of person who could have fallen into these errors would be one who was completely unlettered and unskilled in both profane and sacred literature. Philo Judaeus, therefore, whose talent, erudition, and eloquence were celebrated in antiquity, was not the author of this book but some person devoid of artistry, eloquence, talent, and letters. In no place certainly does this false Philo platonize, but speaks everywhere not only ignorantly and haltingly, but without any cultivation or adornment." *De locis theologicis*, p. 233.

[33] It is possible that some of this is owing to the influence of Valla. But since the technique of philological criticism is used very widely by the humanists, a direct filiation might be difficult to trace.

[34] *De institutione historiae universae*, p. 86.

[35] The assimilation of a historical "inquest" to a hearing of oral testimony is suggested by the practice of Thucydides and strongly confirmed by the theoretical prescriptions of Polybius. And although it obviously assumes that all historiography is contemporary history, the convention is so strong that it is unthinkingly applied to the general practice of all historians on the part of writers of the sixteenth century

out, *viva voce* evidence is normally demanded because it
can be subjected to direct interrogation; in history, conversely, and "especially in one which is not of our age,"
the characteristic form of information is a "testimony" not
a "testifier." [36] But although written information is peculiarly historical, it is not necessarily ruled out of court. Indeed, in the special case of public records, it is not only
admitted by the lawyer, but may even be preferred to oral
testimony.[37] The evidence of history, accordingly, may be
justified by legal practice. But this is only on condition that
it conform to the rules on written instruments. And hence
at this juncture the focus of Baudouin's argument shifts
from the apologetic to the critical.

The rule of courts, he notes, is that when the statement
of a witness is read, and not delivered orally, it must be
presented verbatim and intact, since any alteration or sup-
pression would amount to a dictation of his testimony. For
somewhat similar reasons, furthermore, it is equally a rule
of law that in the probation of contracts, wills, and other
acts, the autograph is better than a copy and must alone be
used if it is extant.[38] And his inference from these to history is the complete exclusion of "derivative accounts" in
favor of the "source" or archetype. "The jurisconsults, certainly, when it is a matter of the faith and probity of instruments, do not stop at what are called exemplars, but
require the *authentica* or 'archetypes.' And shall we, in the
question of some ancient history, prefer more recent witnesses to those who were very ancient, and classic, so to
speak? And shall a secondary and interpolated narrative be
of greater credit than the first and the intact?" [39] In the

who are clearly admitting secondary writers of a later date. So, for example, Cano, *De locis theologicis*, p. 238. Baudouin, to my knowledge,
is the first to break with this convention deliberately.

[36] Baudouin, *De institutione historiae universae*, p. 90.

[37] *Ibid.*, pp. 90–91.   [38] *Ibid.*, pp. 92–93, 99–100.   [39] *Ibid.*, p. 93.

elaboration of this point, moreover, there is a movement of Baudouin's thought from the construction of a formal parallel to the more general ground on which the rule is based. "But again I say that the newer and more recent a narration of the past, the more mendacious it normally becomes. For as wine grows weaker the more it is diluted, and at last becomes devoid of taste, and as a rumor, the longer it progresses, recedes even further from the truth and constantly increases in its falsity, so a history, which has been tossed about in many repetitions, and besprinkled with the words of many versions, will often be at last contaminated, and thus degenerate to fable." [40] The underlying principle, accordingly, is drawn from the psychology of rumor, and with this more general reflection the rule against derivative accounts is stated in an even clearer form. Against the danger of degenerated narratives, "it is an easy caution," says Baudouin, "if we go back to the authors who were first, and tolerate no rivulets recently drawn off in substitution for the very sources." [41]

Through all of this discussion, finally, it is explicitly assumed that an "archetype" or "author who was first" is a prime observer or a near equivalent, the legal analogue for which is the rule excluding hearsay testimony. A historical authority, accordingly, is one who was close to the event, and, strictly speaking, literally present.[42] But there are cases of necessity, Baudouin observes, in which even hearsay is admissible in court. And in history as well one may resort to "witnesses of secondary rank" if no other alternative exists, if the author is especially judicious, and if he is not too distant from the happening.[43] This latter class, it may

---

[40] *Ibid.*, p. 94.   [41] *Ibid.*, p. 95.

[42] "I should prefer, indeed, that all historians be narrating things which they have seen and at which they were present." *Ibid.*, p. 91.

[43] "But if there occur no authors who were eyewitnesses and could be called *autoptai*, we should listen next to those who narrate what they

be noted, is similarly justified in present practice, especially for ancient history, where true originals are relatively scarce.[44]

Taken as a whole, it is surely fair to say that these conceptions of Baudouin are the beginnings of an operationally significant distinction between original and secondary documents.[45] But the limitations, nonetheless, are still very numerous and great. Baudouin, to begin with, does not distinguish, in the general class of original materials, between original narrative relations, in which events are consciously interpreted, and documentary records or "remains," in which transactions are more likely to be noted unreflectively, and hence often with more reliability. It is true, of course, that, like Bodin and other authors of the period, he is enormously impressed by "public monuments," by which are meant official records. And there is reason to believe that this esteem is partially inspired by an intuition of the documentary aspect which many such materials present.[46]

took from others in good faith, and especially so if the period of these, as well as their antiquity and virtue, commend their authority and faith. Seneca says that those who admit that they have not seen themselves, but affirm that they have heard from others, are witnesses of second rank. But even these are not always rejected by the jurisconsults." *Ibid.*, pp. 91–92.

[44] So Ernst Bernheim, *Lehrbuch*, p. 413; and see V. Langlois and C. Seignobos, *Introduction to the Study of History*, pp. 179, 184.

[45] As already indicated the Polybian principle of "autopsy," although suggestive and somewhat similar, cannot really be regarded as a precedent for this. The distinction is between a rule in favor of eye-witness oral testimony as opposed to documents in general and a rule concerning the relative weight of two classes of documents. Thus, again, the importance of Baudouin's recognition that oral testimony is rare in history, that it deals with "documents," not "testifiers." It should also be noted that Bernheim (*Lehrbuch*, p. 488), is either too hasty or too vague in his suggestion that the distinction emerges very late. The development is obviously highly complicated. And it will not be fully understood until the history of historical methodology becomes subject to further research.

[46] See especially his discussion of Roman archives and public records, *De institutione historiae universae*, pp. 134–37.

For the theory of history, however, the important point is that this element is not yet grasped. The official monuments are generally regarded by Baudouin as narrative in different form.[47] And insofar as he accords them special status, the ground is not the distinction between documentary remains and narrative relation but between a publicly attested history and a version which is merely private.[48] For the sixteenth century, therefore, the ideal type of source is still the literary narrative.

With respect to this, moreover, Baudouin is implicitly assuming that the discrimination between the older and the later narrative, as well as the determination of the prime observer, is always immediately given.[49] This, however, can often be established only by a systematic comparison of versions, since sources sometimes come undated and the relations of dependent testimonies are very frequently complex. Moreover, with this technique of source analysis, it is sometimes possible to reconstruct a lost original by the conflation of derivative accounts.

It may also be that on the use of secondary statements,

---

[47] See below, pp. 134 ff.

[48] In the sixteenth century public records are normally regarded as perpetual annals in which the recording of all significant occurrences is the official charge of special commissioners, preferably priests. The official, sometimes sacerdotal, status, together with the fact that they are "open to inspection," is what gives them special credibility. For indications of this idea in Josephus and Agrippa, see above, p. 91, n. 4; in Patrizzi, see above, p. 98; in Cano, see *De locis theologicis*, p. 231; in Bodin, see *Methodus*, p. 126B. There are many examples in Baudouin, but the clearest, perhaps, is the following comment on the public archives of the early Christian Church: "But in this matter of preserving the history of things, I especially regret that the ancient custom of the Christians is not observed. The Church of old had its chosen actuaries (to use a term of law), who were diligently to collect the memory of these affairs in *bona fides* and to record them by public authority; and such monuments of uncorrupted faith were kept safely in its archives, although open for everyone to see." *De institutione historiae universae*, pp. 133–34.

[49] See below, p. 132, n. 51.

where no original is extant, Baudouin's standards are too lax. If the author was a "good" historian, it is assumed, without demand for further inquiry, that he was careful in the use of sources. In principle, however, the statements of a secondary author are not to be considered under modern standards unless his source can be properly identified and its competence and biases assessed. But in the majority of cases this is little better than an educated guess, and although the differences are great in theory, the modern practice, I suspect, is not far removed from the standards of Baudouin.[50]

Baudouin, finally, is implicitly assuming that the distinction between prime and derivative accounts is an aspect of entire works, as though the whole of any secondary history were directly borrowed from a single older version and so on back to the "first and the intact." [51] But a derivative account may sometimes be composed from several sources, and even in contemporary narratives the individual assertions may often be derivative, so that, strictly speaking,

[50] Thus, for instance, the "divinatory" element in the reconstructions of early Roman history from later sources by Niebuhr and Mommsen. See E. A. Freeman's introduction to T. H. Mommsen, *History of Rome*, pp. xi ff.

[51] The entire spirit of Baudouin's notions as to how the sources actually present themselves, how works are related, and how they ought to be compared, is best revealed by the following passage: "Nor do I take it ill if there be many writers on some one event. On the contrary, I wish there might be many to compare, for I know how useful this comparison may be. But I should like them to be such as are serious and just in their authority. And I hold that those are to be studied in the first place, whom the later historians have followed; and what the latter have added to the former is then, I think, to be discriminated. And so my desire, I should say, is this: that the very oldest authors be read first, but afterwards the one who is closest to these first in age, and then each one in his place and order, if he be not unworthy of a hearing; and that what the later have added to the earlier be noted. For the condition with history is much the same as with a rumor; small from fear at the beginning, it grows as it progresses, says the poet." *De institutione historiae universae*, pp. 94–95.

the distinction between original and secondary should be applied to statements, not to entire works. From the standpoint of entire works, moreover, the very concept of a source or archetype is subject to a minor ambiguity, for there is a certain sense in which the model for later imitations, although itself composed of older elements, may be called the archetype of all its copies. A good example of a "source" in this respect would be the extant books of Livy which were widely copied in the Renaissance.

Important as they are, however, these limitations of Baudouin's doctrine are either omissions of technical refinements or crudities in formulation which do not affect the basic insight. And taken together with the other tests of authenticity, his views on sources are part of an impressive system of external or preliminary criticism. What Cano and Baudouin clearly recognize is that before the *bona fides* of an author may be advanced in confirmation of assertions, it must first be shown that the history in question is his own, and, for Baudouin in addition, that the version is complete and accurate, and that the author was a prime observer or a near equivalent.

The final section of Baudouin's oration is an attempt to demonstrate that the sources of a universal history are not only reasonably honest, but are available for every period, and in quantities sufficient for a knowledge of details.[52] The claim, of course, is over-optimistic. But in the course of his apologetic, nonetheless, two conceptions are advanced which are of great importance for a doctrine of heuristic, or a method of collecting information. The occasion for the first of these is Baudouin's recognition of the fact that in many periods the keeping of records was deficient, and

[52] "This only . . . have I wished to say, that the writers are not lacking, nor the monuments, nor memory, nor light—and not even in the darker times—for us to pursue what we have undertaken in good hope." *Ibid.*, p. 163.

that in the course of time, moreover, a great deal of information had been lost.[53] And his principle, in answer to this scarcity, is a systematic method of research, a thorough collection and assemblage of all existing scraps of information. "Of whatever sort the remnants left us," says Baudouin, "(for once again this must be said) they can be conflated, in one way or another, into a history sufficiently entire, if in searching out the different elements in different authors, we thoroughly investigate them all, and collect and aptly join together what each individual provides. For I confess that both diligence in searching is required, and a certain art in using what is found." [54]

The second principle, which is closely related to the first, is that the presentation of events and actions need not have been intended as a "history," but that many authors "who apparently are doing something else, will be doing this if we make use of them correctly." [55] The idea, in other words, is that the search for historical materials must not be limited to the formal literary narrative. The letters of Cicero, in Baudouin's favorite example, contain innumerable judgments of persons and events which are scattered fragments, so to speak, of a contemporary history of Rome.[56] And in the form of enrichments and corrections

[53] A constantly repeated theme. See especially *ibid.*, p. 124, where Baudouin sees the history of history as a constant war between "oblivion" and "memory": "I do not know whether to lament the monuments which perished, or hail the ones which have survived. But pleasing to admire is the extraordinary providence of God, by which it has transpired that the memory of things gone by has been preserved in many forms."

[54] *Ibid.*, p. 143. See also pp. 123, 141.

[55] *Ibid.*, p. 116. See also p. 121: "Moreover, just as I say that very rich and ample material for history is to be discovered in the books of Cicero, so also there are accounts of many great events, which would otherwise escape us, to be excerpted from other writers' commentaries, even if they do not profess themselves historians."

[56] The methodological significance of these letters as "historical equivalents" is elaborately discussed, *ibid.*, pp. 116–21. Cicero, he tries to show,

they may be conflated with a narrative tradition which without them would be arid and uncertain.[57] "And not only from the letters," says Baudouin, "but from Cicero's speeches and his other commentaries we may extract, I think, a brilliant emendation of the history of Rome." [58]

The preceding concepts, obviously, are the first reflection in the theory of history of that vast expansion in the range of sources which is ever more characteristic of contemporary scholarship.[59] And in the illustration of these principles there is a survey of the range of sources in which all these elements are catalogued. The forms of history, according to Baudouin, include not only the formal literary narrative, but the letters of a public figure; forensic speeches, and even panegyrics, on occasion, if their biases are cautiously discounted; [60] paintings, tapestries, and statues (in the sense of graphic narratives); numismatic and memorial inscriptions; [61] legal codes and statutes; songs and epics (in

---

had once composed a history of Rome for the era of his consulship which apparently was never published. But there is no reason to lament, Baudouin argues, since the letters are "virtually" that history. "Great, therefore, the damage in its loss. But cannot that exposition of the history of Rome be found in one way or another in the rest of his writings which survive?" *Ibid.*, pp. 118–19.

[57] *Ibid.*, p. 119.

[58] *Ibid.*, p. 120.

[59] Above all in antiquarian research, of which the greatest French examples are Budé for classical antiquity, and Etienne Pasquier for French antiquities. Classical scholarship was by far the more developed, and Baudouin is thoroughly familiar with it as one aspect of his legal studies.

[60] This is the one occasion where Baudouin is aware that these "other" forms of history have critical problems peculiar to their functions. In the case of speeches, especially funeral orations, the question is forced on him because these were a classic example of historical "corruption." He would admit the latter, therefore, only when no other source exists, and with very special care. See *ibid.*, pp. 120–21, 172–73.

[61] The inclusion of the graphic arts is primarily to emphasize the point that history may occur in any form (*ibid.*, pp. 31–33, 122), and although Baudouin gives many illustrations their use is mainly hypothetical. Coins and inscriptions, however, are occasionally mentioned as sources by the ancients and were used extensively by Budé among others. The citation

the sense of oral "histories"); [62] priestly chronicles and annals; and, finally, archives and official records, ecclesiastical as well as civil, which are valued above all the rest as "history" attested publicly.[63] As already indicated, the use of these materials is still implicitly regarded as a mere enrichment of the narrative tradition. And they are considered in theory at least, not as the documentary remains of an event, but as narratives in fragmentary form. Apart from this, however, the illustrations and suggestions of Baudouin are the foundations of a doctrine of heuristic—for his definition of a source is comprehensive, and he has a definite conception of the function of research.

---

of the graphic arts is also used by Patrizzi, *Dialogue* IV, pp. 429–30, to illustrate the point that historiography is any form of sense-memory.

[62] He thinks of these, in other words, not as documentary indications of a people's psyche, but as real historical traditions. This, of course, is extremely over-optimistic. But Baudouin does not consider the problem since his major purpose in this context (*De institutione historiae universae*, pp. 125–28) is to prove, apologetically, that historical traditions go back to the "beginning." His point, therefore, is that the earliest tradition is always oral in its form, and is recorded at a later date. This idea, although already suggested in the ancients, is nicely illustrated by the work of Christian missionaries in writing down the epics of the American Indians (*ibid.*, p. 127). But it does not occur to Baudouin to infer that precisely for such reasons the earliest history of any people is suspect.

[63] There is as yet no theoretical distinction between publicly authorized annals, often in the form of priestly chronicles, which record "events" both great and small, and the documentary record of transactions. And this is immediately apparent in his discussion of the Roman "archives" (*ibid.*, pp. 133–37). It is obvious enough, however, that Baudouin has a deep awareness of the value of archival records, and his appeal for the "opening of archives" is uncannily "modern" in its tone (*ibid.*, p. 138). But part of this respect, no doubt, is the result of a naïve belief that official records are completely truthful simply by the virtue of the fact that they are "public." See above, p. 131, n. 48.

IX

JEAN BODIN
THE RULES FOR
TESTING HISTORICAL ASSERTIONS

Comprehensive as they are, however, these achievements of Cano and Baudouin are not as yet a full-scale methodology. The missing element is a doctrine of internal criticism on which Cano is extremely vague and Baudouin completely silent. And the reason, as heretofore suggested, is that from the apologetic standpoint of these authors there is less occasion for particular criteria.

With Bodin, however, the purpose has become more practical. The *Methodus*, in contrast to Baudouin's oration, is not so much a preamble to the art of reading, as a handbook of advice to students on how to read historians with profit.[1] Therefore, in addition to a plan of study—with re-

[1] Bodin's thoughts are too diffuse for summary. It may be noted, however, that it is not quite justifiable to say with J. G. A. Pocock, in *The Ancient Constitution and the Feudal Law* (p. 11), that the work is hopelessly eclectic in its aim, or with Moreau-Reibel, in *Jean Bodin et le droit publique* (pp. 69 ff.), that it was intended mainly as a philosophy of history, or with writers of the seventeenth and eighteenth centuries that it rapidly turns into a mere treatise on public law. No doubt the work exhibits all these characteristics. But it is clear enough that it was consciously intended as a method of reading for the student, and that it is the first elaboration of all the issues which contemporaries were beginning to identify as belonging to that method. In addition to an opening preamble on the value and the scope of history, the *Methodus* falls into four main classes of topics. One, taken over from Vives and perfected,

flections on the course of history and canons of interpretation in the form of generalizations on society and politics—there is a detailed exposition of the literature, which includes not only a catalogue of authors but also a critical essay on historians in which a great number of writers are individually described.[2] In the evaluation of the latter, therefore, a number of standards are suggested both for the identification of a good historian and for determining the circumstances under which he may be trusted. And in the introduction to the chapter there is a summation of these rules and standards which is in effect a method of internal criticism.[3]

The initial aspect of Bodin's prescriptions is certain general characteristics of an author's background, style,

---

is a comprehensive catalogue of narrative historians systematically and chronologically arranged—and hence a kind of "practical heuristic." A second element is a "plan" of reading which, merely exhortative in Vives and Baudouin, here becomes a "scheme" of history, with the rise and fall of peoples in a southeast-northwest procession as the organizing line of movement. And clustered around this we have, in addition to a system of chronology, philosophicohistorical elucidations and defenses of the scheme such as the demonstration of the genealogical continuity of peoples, the refutation of the four monarchies, and the refutation of the "law" of historical decadence. A third element, unique with Bodin, is a method of interpretation consisting of his theory of the influence of climate and other geographical factors on the "natural character" of peoples, and his system of public law which includes brief surveys of the constitutional history of all the major states in history. Connected with these is his list of categories presented as a scheme for taking notes. Equally unique, and for our interest decisive, is the fourth element—a critical evaluation of the narrative tradition.

[2] This series of portraits and commentaries also deals with the major topics covered by a writer, a listing of his extant works, etc., and hence, although not organized chronologically, it may be regarded as a first essay in the history of history, anterior by several years to that of T. Voisin de la Popelinière, *Histoire des histoires* (Paris, 1599).

[3] Bodin, of course, introduces this discussion with a refutation of the skeptics, and a statement of the logic of historical belief. But since these remarks are scattered and cryptic we have mentioned them in the course of our discussion of Cano and Baudouin. See above, p. 109, n. 17; p. 111, n. 24; p. 112; p. 120, n. 14.

and information which seem related to his value as a source. And his positions here are a restatement, with significant additions, of what was beginning to be known as the "standard of Polybius." [4] The first requirement is that since the better part of history is politics, the good historian must be familiar with the principles of statecraft. And this, in agreement with Polybius, is most readily acquired from actual participation in command or counsel. But for Bodin as a jurist and comparative historian there are other criteria as well. Training in the law is an alternative, because it is from the laws and customs of a people that the real foundations of its state are understood.[5] And since "the very difficult science of government is scarcely to be learned . . . [without] a varied knowledge of all the different peoples," [6] the extensive reading of historians is not only a valuable supplement to practical experience but may even be sufficient in itself.[7]

[4] This celebration of Polybius is a sharp reaction to the confusion of history and rhetoric in the older humanist tradition. Among practicing historians, of course, the change is signalized by the "realistic" manner of Machiavelli and Guiccardini. Among the theorists, however, the change comes somewhat later, and is first encountered in the sharp distinction between history as fact and history as literature in both Baudouin and Patrizzi. Both authors depend on Polybius' authority; and one manifesto of the new approach is Uberto Foglietta, *De norma polybiana, Artis historicae penus*, II. In all these writers, however, the major point is a definition of the proper "aim" of history as concerned with "facts" and not with "words." But in Bodin we have a complete, and fully independent, evaluation of the Polybian criteria of objectivity.

[5] "But it is not simply by participation in command or public counsels, but from adjudications most especially that the customs of the different peoples and the forms of commonwealth are learned." *Methodus*, p. 125A. Cf. the contrasting position of Polybius in this typical passage: "So I should say that history will never be properly written, until either men of action undertake to write it . . . or historians become convinced that practical experience is of the first importance for historical composition." *Histories* xii, 28.

[6] *Methodus*, p. 125A.

[7] The very best historian is one who "has united extensive erudition and a knowledge of the public law with practical experience" (*ibid.*, p. 125A). And there have been closet scholars, of such enormous industry

The good historian, moreover, must be reliably informed
as to the facts, which means, according to Polybius, that
he must have either witnessed them himself or directly
questioned persons who were present.[8] In Bodin too, of
course, contemporary authors may very well be "good."
But the best, he feels, have been neither too early nor too
late,[9] since a historian of somewhat later date is in a better
position to speak frankly and is somewhat less suscepti-
ble to bias than one who was too close to the event.[10] The
very best, moreover, have very often had the viewpoint of
a foreigner, since on institutional details at least, which
are the things of greatest value in a history, the foreign
author is often more informative than natives who tend
to pass over such matters as self-evident.[11] And hence his
image of a well-informed authority is less the indefatigable
on-the-spot inquirer than the somewhat more detached

---

in reading history, that they "have equalled those who spent their entire
life in governing the commonwealth" (*ibid.*, p. 125A). This, of course,
is a deliberate departure from Polybius who was a bitter enemy of
"book-learning"; see *Histories* xii, 25: "And when history is written by
the book-learned, without technical knowledge, and without clearness of
detail, the work loses all value." The complaint, however, against book-
learning as a form of "training" is never clearly distinguished in Polybius' mind from the complaint against writing history from documentary records.

It may be noted also that Bodin's idea that the ideal background for
an historian is a combination of theory and practice is in direct parallel
to his portrait of the ideal jurisconsult.

[8] The most famous statement is *Histories* xii, 27. But here again Polybius cannot fully distinguish between the evils of history written from
documents, and the naïveté of historians trained from books.

[9] *Methodus*, p. 126A.   [10] *Ibid.*, p. 127A.

[11] This idea is strongly emphasized in explaining why the Greek historians of Rome are more informative than Latin writers. The comparative standpoint is the stated reason. And the best of all is Dionysius of
Halicarnassus because he has an enormous interest in institutions and
customs which the Latins neglected as too commonplace. "And this we
see has affected almost all historians, that they omit the commonplace
institutions of a commonwealth, as if known just as well to foreigners
as natives, or as if they thought that they would never change." *Ibid.*,
pp. 131B–132A.

historian who has diligently consulted records, especially the "public monuments."

With Bodin, accordingly, the idea of a critical secondary author is slowly beginning to emerge.[12] And there is already a suggestion that among the tests for judging any author is an investigation of his habits of research—his willingness to go to sources and his sense of obligation in reporting them correctly.[13] But although the use of what are implicitly conceived to be original materials[14] is a

---

[12] Baudouin, for example, thinks of secondary history as so imitative that he has serious doubts whether history should ever be rewritten. He generally concludes that "we ought to be reciters rather than new authors" (*De institutione historiae universae*, p. 99), and Livy is commended for having plagiarized Polybius verbatim, since the source is thereby undisturbed (*ibid.*, p. 98). See also *ibid.*, p. 95. The clearest contrast in Bodin to this, however, is the following comment on Dionysius of Halicarnassus: "And his credibility is even more than the others' because he wrote of a foreign state and not his own, and collected commentaries from every quarter, and especially the secrets of the state from public records." *Methodus*, p. 126A. These differences, however, are only tendencies which neither author follows up.

[13] The best example is his evaluation of Guiccardini: "In him, moreover, there is a remarkable industry in searching out the truth. He accepted nothing rashly, but confirmed everything with necessary arguments. For it is reported that he drained and sifted his information from the very sources, from letters, statutes, treatises, and speeches. . . . Indeed, he was so diligent an investigator of persons, places, and events, as well as of stratagems and deeds, that he seems to have inspected all the cities, towns, camps, and rivers of Italy, and the public records also, which, in my opinion, are the thing of most importance." *Ibid.*, p. 136B. There is also a lengthy list of historians "good" in this respect, i.e., from the standpoint of their diligence. See *ibid.*, pp. 126A–126B. And in his portraits of individual historians a judgment of their practice is frequently included—e.g., his favorable comments on Polybius (p. 130B), Dionysius of Halicarnassus and Dio Cassius (p. 133A), and his negative comments on Giovio (pp. 130B–131A), and perhaps Bembo (p. 137A). It is obvious enough, however, that in most cases these evaluations are superficial or naïve. There is rarely any serious attempt to prove the judgment by testing an author's use of sources with respect to specific statements, and systematically throughout his work. Moreover, in his eulogies at least, Bodin is normally taking the writer's own statement of his practice pretty much at face value. Hence his overestimation of Dionysius of Halicarnassus.

[14] This is clear enough in the comment on Guiccardini in the above

basic obligation of the writer, a return to "authors who were first" is not demanded of the critic or the student. And in this respect the precautions of Baudouin are ignored, since the critical secondary author is tacitly admitted as a source. It should be pointed out, however, that the suggestions of Bodin in other areas are little affected by this error. With one exception, his tests of objectivity are either intended for contemporary sources or are generally applicable to these.

The good historian, furthermore, must not only be informed and critical, but must be willing to report his knowledge honestly. And the *prima facie* evidence for this is the manner of his presentation. A historian is suspect, for example, if he is excessively eulogistic or censorious, for since the vast majority of actors are neither wholly good nor wholly bad, unmitigated praise or blame is less the mark of a historian than of an orator who pleads a cause.[15] This, and similar objections to moralizing or dramatic history, have once again been inspired by Polybius, and are standard in the later sixteenth century. But Bodin advances to the view that value judgments be eliminated altogether.[16] The argument, anticipating Ranke's, is that such statements, on the one hand, are superfluous, since the bare nar-

---

note. And it is especially clear in the following: "Little to be trusted are those narratives, indeed, whose authors take everything from hearsay, from the talk of others, as Polybius has said, and have not consulted public records." *Ibid.*, p. 126A. The implication here, however, is never actually articulated.

[15] *Ibid.*, p. 125B.

[16] Of this departure Bodin is highly conscious. There is an elaborate weighing of the pros and cons, and he recognizes that "very serious writers have rendered an opinion on the thing they are expounding." Polybius, he notes, explicitly approved of moral comment. His own preference, however, is for the "nude" and "unadorned" style of Caesar, although he would admit that where an author has some special *expertise* a comment may sometimes be appropriate, if it is done implicitly and cautiously. *Ibid.*, pp. 127B–129A.

ration of the facts is normally sufficient to convey their implication. A Nero, for example, is so effectively indicted by recital of his crimes, that the appendage of a moralizing comment would even diminish the dramatic impact.[17] On the other hand, the "unasked for" comments of an author arouse suspicion in a cautious reader and cast doubt upon his whole account. For they reveal a desire to impose opinions which may have affected treatment of the facts.[18]

A historian, furthermore, may also be discounted for his style, if his language is poetic and exaggerated, or if he interrupts the sequence of the narrative with entertaining but irrelevant digressions. In all such cases, holds Bodin, he reveals that he is writing to give pleasure. And "I have come to the conclusion," he asserts, "that it is utterly impossible for him who writes to entertain, to give the truth of the events as well, which is what Thucydides, Plutarch, and Diodorus censure in Herodotus." [19] Here, too, Bodin's

---

[17] "And although many think that eulogizations of the good and vituperations of the bad contribute to the usefulness of history, this can be more truthfully and better done by the philosophers, whose special task it is, than by historians. And yet more than enough does he vituperate a Nero who narrates that he murdered very honorable men, his tutor, two wives, his brother Britannicus, and finally his mother. All of these are written by Suetonius with purity, simplicity, and without exaggerated images. But when Appian wrote that Mithridates murdered his mother, his brother, his three little sons, and as many daughters, he added: 'Bloody and cruel was he to all.' By these latter words he undermined his credit no less than Giovio did his, when in a long oration he elaborated on all the cruelties of Selim, ruler of the Turks, with the highest images of scorn." *Ibid.*, p. 128B. As in Ranke, therefore, the idea is not that values are relative, but that direct expression of a value judgment is inappropriate to the task of a historian.

[18] "For since history ought to be nothing but the image of the truth, and as though a public record of *res gestae* put forward in the clearest light for everyone to judge, antecedent judgment by historians detracts very greatly from the facts, because they apparently wish to seize the minds of inexperienced readers for dubious opinions. But to cautious readers, who do not wish to be deceived, they are suspect for this very fact, that they give an unsolicited opinion." *Ibid.*, p. 127A.

[19] *Ibid.*, p. 129A.

position is unusually advanced in that he recommends, implicitly at least, the complete elimination of invented speeches.[20]

These first criteria are still intended by Bodin for the judgment of the author as a whole, and not of his particular assertions. But even so, the Polybian rule, as he elaborates it, is a decided advance upon the moralistic norm of Cano. For Bodin, the indications of a good historian are not simply his "integrity and prudence," but a number of external attributes—the training of an author, his attitude towards sources, and his style—from which these moral

[20] It is very possible that Bodin really thought that he was following Polybius in this, for there are bitter protests in the latter against "implausible" and "arbitrary" speeches. But for Polybius, as for all the ancients, the rewriting of a document attributed to the actor by direct quotation was regarded as a legitimate convention for achieving unity of style. See J. B. Bury, *The Ancient Greek Historians*, p. 230. And even where there was no document, it was a practice equally universal to invent a speech on the basis of indirect reports as to what had actually been said, or a guess as to what could or should have been said in view of the occasion. The meaning of Polybius' protests, therefore, is merely a reaction against the abuses of this license by the rhetoricians— a demand, first, that the substance of the actor's statements should always be preserved in the rewriting, and, second, that the practice of interpolating speeches should be carefully restricted by a scrupulous regard for the probabilities of the occasion. It would seem, however, that Bodin interpreted this conditional attack upon invented speeches as absolute. This is already suggested by the uncompromising language on invented speeches (*fictae conciones*) which appears in his complaints about digressions. But the most decisive indication is his praise for what he rather gullibly believes is Guiccardini's scrupulous fidelity on the matter of direct and indirect quotations: "And so this expression frequently occurs [in him]: 'he spoke in these words' or, if the actual words are missing, 'he spoke to this effect.' In this he proceeds very differently from Giovio who, as with the bulk of all that he reports, invented speeches also or rather declamations in scholastic manner. And the proof of this is that the speech of Baglioni is plainly contrary to that which Guiccardini transcribed from an actual copy." *Ibid.*, p. 136B. Hence the break with Polybius is real if unsuspected. And the ban on invented speeches is the sharpest expression of Bodin's demand for total realism, for it is in advance of the historiographical practice of his time.

qualities may be inferred. And hence, although obviously still too general, they are objective criteria of choice.

But the most far-reaching and decisive innovation is the recognition by Bodin that an author's will to tell the truth will tend to vary with the bearing of his interests. This view depends upon the insight that there are a variety of circumstances in which even good historians are likely to be biased. The love of country, for example, is so pervasive and profound that "no one," thinks Bodin, "is able to forget the praises of his fatherland, or pass over them in calm impartiality." [21] Fabius, for example, "was a man of great integrity and prudence from whom no plans of the Republic or the enemy were hidden," and yet his version of the Punic War was slanted in favor of the Romans.[22]

[21] *Ibid.*, p. 127B.

[22] *Ibid.*, p. 125B. The reference is to Polybius' criticism of Fabius, the Roman, and Philinus, the Carthaginian, who had written on the Punic Wars. And it may well be that the following passage was suggestive to Bodin in his movement towards a psychological perspective: "Now judging from their [Fabius' and Philinus'] lives and principles, I do not suppose that these writers have intentionally stated what was false; but I think that they are much in the same state of mind as men in love. Partisanship and complete prepossession made Philinus think that all the actions of the Carthaginians were characterised by wisdom, honour, and courage: those of the Romans by the reverse. Fabius thought the exact opposite." Polybius, *Histories* i, 14. The implication, therefore, is that there are certain situations in which bias is normally beyond control, so that the problem of criticism would be psychological as well as moral. But the grasping of this implication is Bodin's and not Polybius'. The purpose of the latter is simply a moralistic warning to the future writer. "Now in other relations of life," he continues, "one would hesitate to exclude such warmth of sentiment: for a good man ought to be loyal to his friends and patriotic to his country; ought to be at one with his friends in their hatreds and their likings. But directly a man assumes the moral attitude of an historian he ought to forget all considerations of that kind." It is not, of course, that Bodin is more sophisticated than Polybius, but that he is now concerned, for the first time, with the norms of criticism and not the canons of a good historian, with the problem of how historians actually behave and not what their practice ought to be.

And Polybius himself, observes Bodin, "who of all the best writers is considered the most truthful," was not impartial in discussing Megalopolis.[23]

Similar biases, moreover, must be expected from the ties of interest, as when the author is himself an actor or is writing of his party or his friends. And where religious differences are present the likelihood is even stronger. "It is inadvisable," Bodin points out, "to seek the opinion of the pagans on the Jews, or of the Jews about the Christians, or even our own as to the Moors and Mohammedans, since the most bitter enmities of men are those of disagreement on religion."[24] Here too, as in the case of patriotic bias, it need not be assumed that distortions are deliberate, since the author may be blinded by his prejudice, especially in olden times when "each of the peoples was uninformed on the antiquities of others."[25]

On almost any topic, finally, the truthfulness of history is suspect if the author had reason to be fearful. The publication of the truth, for instance, may be offensive to powerful contemporaries.[26] And the threat is all the more enhanced where the reputation of the ruler is at stake and the commonwealth in question is despotic. In all such cases, thinks Bodin, the facts will be distorted or suppressed. "For who," he asks, "will expect the truth to be given by historians in a state where to say what one does not wish is disgraceful; what one wishes unfortunate and dangerous?"[27] His illustration here is Tacitus' complaint on the decline of honesty in Roman history which accompanied the growth of despotism.

Bodin, accordingly, is willing to concede to skepticism a

[23] *Methodus*, p. 127B. "For when it was a question of his own countrymen, he could not refrain from a bitter attack upon Phylarchus for concealing the virtue and bravery of the Megalopolitans in the war against Aristomachus."

[24] *Ibid.*, p. 127A.   [25] *Ibid.*   [26] *Ibid.*, p. 126A.   [27] *Ibid.*

variety of common circumstances in which bias may almost always be expected, and several of his findings are reminiscent of Agrippa and Patrizzi. The difference now, however, is that these biases are no longer understood as indications of complete depravity and as the sole motivations from which history is written, but are psychologically interpreted as normal and discountable. This is the idea, for instance, in Bodin's defense of Tacitus against those who would strike him from the list of good historians on the basis of his anti-Christian animus. Since the Christians, says Bodin, were a universally defamed minority at the time when Tacitus was writing, his contempt was natural enough, and cannot be taken as proof of his depravity. Moreover, since Tacitus was born a pagan, in a pagan era, his opposition to Christianity was not only natural but pious, and might even be taken as sign of moral virtue.[28] Bodin's

[28] "Budé has bitterly characterized Tacitus as the most wicked writer of them all because he wrote some things against the Christians. And this is the reason, I believe, why Tertullian called him most deceitful, Orosius, a flatterer. But as the jurisconsult Marcellus replied that a prostitute, by being such, did basely, but granted that she was such, didn't, so also it was impious of Tacitus not to be a Christian, but not impious for him to write against us, since he was under obligation to the pagan superstition. On the contrary, I should find him truly impious if he did not defend whatever religion he thought true, and try to undermine its adversaries. For since the Christians and the Hebrews were daily dragged to punishment like poisoners and were accused of every indecency and crime, what historian would refrain from terms of scorn? But if ignorance deserves excuse, Tacitus must surely be excused. . . . So also was Suetonius vicious when he wrote of Christians, yet his history is praised so greatly, that in the opinion of impartial judges nothing was ever written more accurately by any historian." *Methodus*, pp. 134B–135A. It may be noted that Baudouin makes a similar argument, on Tacitus as well as others, in his defense of good historians from hypercriticism. "It is true that Tertullian, an austere and serious writer, said that Tacitus was full of lies. But this he said only when the issue was of Jewish history, and here we too would say that Tacitus spoke nonsense. But what has that to do with Roman subjects?" *De institutione historiae universae*, pp. 77–78. With Baudouin, however, this is only a passing thought which does not issue in an investigation of the rules of criticism.

idea, accordingly, is that no historian is wholly good or
bad, but that his proclivity to bias, or his lack of it, will
tend to vary, in different situations, with the bearing of
his interests and attitudes. And his implicit answer to the
skeptics, therefore, as well as his criterion for judging
sources, gives another set of typical conditions in which
the tendency to bias is discountable.

Bias, to begin with, is not very likely to be present where
interest is not involved at all so that, other factors being
equal, the best historian on any topic is an author who be-
longed to neither party. Dionysius of Halicarnassus, for
example, is more to be trusted on the history of Rome
than Cato, Fabius, or Sallust because he is writing, as Bodin
naïvely thinks, from the "neutral" standpoint of a Greek
and a foreigner.[29] "I do not want," he says, "either domestic judgments or the enemy's, but the verdict of some
third, as in the law, who may be free of all emotion." [30]
This test of interest, moreover, applies not only to the
choice of authors, depending on the nature of the topic,
but also to the choice of topics, depending on the nature
of the author. The narratives of kings, for instance, are
not to be accepted "when they are boastfully speaking of
themselves." But they are quite reliable, according to Bodin,
on certain basic civil institutions "which pertain not at all
or only slightly to their glory or their blame, such as the
system of chronology, the provinces, the public powers,
the ages and succession of the kings, and all such public
calculations in which the secrets of the state lie hidden."[31]
But even when the author is a partisan, he is not necessarily mendacious. He may sometimes overcome his biases;

[29] *Methodus*, p. 125B. See also p. 127B: "And so I willingly assent to
Caesar writing of the customs of the Gauls, or to Tacitus on the Germans, or to Polybius on the Romans, or to Ammianus on the Franks,
since all of them were foreigners. . . ."

[30] *Ibid.*, p. 125B.   [31] *Ibid.*, p. 126B.

and there is a presumptive likelihood of this when he makes admissions in conflict with his interests. "We must be very cautious," says Bodin, "lest we too easily accept a writer on things which do credit to himself, his countrymen, and friends, or which are written to the enemy's disgrace. But as to those deeds, conversely, held to have been done gloriously and nobly by enemies, there is very little doubt as to good faith." [32] Bodin is shrewd enough to recognize that historians are sometimes bribed and that his rule is therefore not infallible.[33] But the more subtle forms of flattery escape him, as when the power of an enemy is magnified in order to enhance a victory or to remove the sting from a defeat.

The converse exception is an author of such perfect faith that whatever his original connections he may be regarded as virtually a neutral.[34] This faith, apparently, is to be established partly from his style, and partly from his reputation. But the sources of the latter are not the general tradition, as in Cano, for they are explicitly restricted to the judgments of contemporaries.[35] And even these, he indicates, must be evaluated in relation to their biases. "For when the Athenians complained that Thucydides wrote many things in favor of the Spartans, they bore great witness to this writer's truthfulness." [36]

There are cases, furthermore, in which partisans of either side have written of the same affairs, so that even if the biases of both be great the truth may be arrived at by comparison. Bodin, unfortunately, is rather cryptic on this

[32] *Ibid.*, p. 125B.
[33] "What we have said about the writings of an enemy is relevant, therefore, unless he is a deserter corrupted and suborned by money, as was Froissart in some people's opinion, the question being who owed more, the English to him, or he to the English, since he openly confessed that he had received the greatest rewards from them. *Ibid.*, pp. 127A–127B.
[34] *Ibid.*, p. 127A.   [35] *Ibid.*, p. 129A.   [36] *Ibid.*

point, and seems to be assuming, quite naïvely, that the truth will be the mean of the extremes. But in the course of his attack on "orators" the principle itself is clearly stated. "The prudent judge," he cautions, "in examining the record of a man will weigh not only the praises of his countrymen and friends but also the statements of his enemies." [37]

An author's truthfulness, however, may be affected not only by attachment to a cause, but also by his fear of consequences. And the principle of caution, in this latter case, is the bearing of his published statements on the interests of powerful contemporaries. Since the danger of offending is greatest on contemporary subjects, there is little reason for suspicion on this score where an author, well informed from documents, has written on a topic in the past. But even on contemporary policies, servility is less to be expected where the commonwealth is nondespotic. And it may even be discounted altogether if an author's memoirs of the present were written mainly for posterity and were intended to be published at some future date.[38]

Bodin is cognizant, moreover, that the pressure of contemporaries may also work the other way, and that publication, where interested witnesses exist, may sometimes be a deterrent to lying. Thus, from the bearing of his interests alone, it might be properly assumed that Caesar, in the Gallic Wars, exaggerated the dimensions of his victories. But according to the Portian Law the penalty for false report of casualties was deprivation of the triumph and *imperium* on which Caesar set so high a store. And al-

[37] *Ibid.*, p. 125B.

[38] "It is better, therefore, all fear removed, to commit writings on present matters to posterity, or if there is someone who prefers to enjoy the glory of his labors in his lifetime, let him write about the actions of a former age, by collecting all the private and the public records as well as what survives in the report of older men." *Methodus*, p. 126A.

though the Portian Law was often broken with impunity, "a man so covetous of glory" would surely be restrained by "fear of infamy," and "especially so because he allowed his writings to be published in his lifetime, and had innumerable enemies who would have been able to demonstrate the lie." The idea, accordingly, is that, by the very nature of his public, the natural temptation to exaggerate was neutralized in Caesar's mind by the disadvantages of probable exposure. And under these conditions, "what he wrote about his wars is considered for the most part to be true." [39]

Despite a certain crudity and lack of order, these critical suggestions of Bodin are a clear theoretical advance beyond the generalities of Cano and Baudouin. For the latter, as for the skeptics, an historian is either "good" or "bad" as such, and his willingness to tell the truth is either to be accepted or rejected as a whole.[40] It is correctly recognized, of course, that a good historian is only a "probable" authority, and that his particular assertions are not to be followed if implausible. But his authority as such, being a judgment of his total personality, creates the same presumption for everything he says. With Bodin, however, the standpoint is more clearly psychological, and there is a corresponding shift of emphasis from the judgment of an author as a whole to an estimation, from the bearing of his interests, of his attitude towards different topics. In other words, the idea of a "choice among historians," of their discrimination into lists of "good" and "bad," is partially transformed into the judgment of specific statements. And to this extent Bodin's warnings on the likelihood of bias approach a genuine system of internal criticism, a list of factors by which an author's willingness to tell the truth

[39] *Ibid.*, p. 127A.
[40] Implications to the contrary in Baudouin are not, as we have seen, developed.

may be inferred for each of his assertions. "It is . . . of no little interest," he says in sum, "whether the historian has written in his works of himself or others, of countrymen or foreigners, of enemies or friends, of military things or civil; and finally whether he has written of his own or of a former age, for his contemporaries or posterity." [41]

With these contributions of Bodin the critical reflections of this early period have been carried to their farthest limit. The main deficiencies are crudities in terms and formulations, a lack of unity and system, and naïveté in the particular examples, defects which are explained, for the most part, by the very newness of the enterprise and a simple lack of information, and also to some extent, I believe, by a subtle limitation of perspective. With the partial exception of Baudouin,[42] the standpoint of these early critics is that of a general reader or historical consumer and not, as in the nineteenth century, that of a professional committed to research. And since their critical needs are therefore less intense, the consequences of their basic insights are not as yet systematically pursued.

Most of the deficiencies, however, are in matters of refinement and detail and not in the ideas themselves. The essential point for the theory of method is that in every area of criticism the beginnings of a doctrine have appeared —a definition of the nature and the range of sources, and a discrimination of original and secondary; a formulation of the logical basis of historical belief and of the conditions for approximating certainty; a method for establishing the authenticity of documents; and a set of psychological criteria for determining the bias of a source. It also should be noted, finally, that these achievements are in no sense

---

[41] *Methodus*, p. 125A.
[42] Who is somewhat more often thinking of a humanist scholar as the typical reader.

archaeological curiosities, but are the actual sources for the subsequent tradition. In the course of the succeeding century the works of all three writers were well known.[43] And Bodin's *Methodus* continued to enjoy a considerable degree of favor as a general handbook for the "art of reading history" despite the fact that in this period there were important methodological advances in certain special areas— as, for example, the work of Mabillon and others in diplomatics.[44] But it is even more important that in the eighteenth century, when the theory of method is again a major interest, it is immediately dependent on the early sources. The most striking evidence of this is the work of Lenglet du Fresnoy, whose *Méthode pour étudier l'histoire* (1713) is adjudged by Bernheim to be "the best methodological handbook of the time." [45] The very title and purpose of this book, an "art of reading" for the cultivated man, is suggestive of Bodin's *Methodus*, which is respectfully cited as its predecessor.[46] In the chapters on the rules of criticism there are not only laudatory citations of the work of Cano, but very considerable stretches which are borrowed directly from Bodin.[47] The dependence is so close, indeed— not only in formulating concepts but even in specific illustrations—that it often passes over into plagiarism.[48] I do not suggest, of course, that there is nothing new in Lenglet du Fresnoy, although there is not as much as might have been

[43] J. L. Brown, *The Methodus ad Facilem Historiarum Cognitionem of Jean Bodin,* p. 195, mentions at least three editions of the *Methodus* in the seventeenth century. In the case of the editions of Cano mentioned by Lang, and of the edition of Baudouin in the eighteenth century, I cannot say, of course, that the historical interest was prime. But that they were well known at least is certain.

[44] See Bernheim, *Lehrbuch,* pp. 220 ff.   [45] *Ibid.,* p. 223.

[46] N. Lenglet du Fresnoy, *A New Method of Studying History,* I, xiii–xiv.

[47] On Cano see *ibid.,* I, 272–73; Bodin forms the basis of two crucial methodological chapters, XVII and XVIII.

[48] This dependency is generally acknowledged, for Du Fresnoy says in the introduction: "From this book I have borrowed what I have thought proper for my design. . . ." *Ibid.,* I, xiv.

expected. My essential point, from the perspective of the history of method, is that the methodological thinking of the eighteenth century, on which the present is itself dependent, is the fruit of a continuous tradition which arises in the later sixteenth century.

Thus in the theory of history as well as in juristic method the later sixteenth century is an epoch of important innovations. In jurisprudence the sovereign authority of Roman Law at last gives way to a comparison and synthesis of the laws of all of the most famous peoples. And in the theory of history the introduction of an art of reading produces the first extensive formulations of the rules and conditions of historical belief. The influence of these accomplishments and even the very fact of their existence have often been obscured by the ahistorical and geometric method which predominates in the succeeding period. And it has sometimes seemed that the comparative approach to legal institutions and the theory of historical criticism are introduced as systematic enterprises only in the eighteenth century. But the truth, as we have tried to show, is that the actual source for both of these developments is the methodological revolution of the later Renaissance. It may be said, indeed, that the deepest aspiration of the later humanists is a union of history and social science, the theoretical influence of which has only begun to be explored.

BIBLIOGRAPHY

I. WORKS OF THE FIFTEENTH AND SIXTEENTH CENTURIES

Agrippa, Henry Cornelius. The Vanity of Arts and Sciences. London and Westminister, 1676.

Annius of Viterbo (Nanni). Berosi . . . antiquitatum Italiae ac totius orbis libri quinque. Antwerp, 1552.

Artis historicae penus. Octodecim scriptorum tam veterum quam recentiorum monumentis et inter eos Ioannis praecipue Bodini libris Methodi instructa, ed. Johann Wolf. 2 vols. Basel, 1579.

Baudouin (Balduinus), François. De institutione historiae universae et ejus cum jurisprudentia conjunctione prolegomenon. Halle, 1726.

Bodin, Jean. Oeuvres philosophiques de Jean Bodin, texts est. and trans. by Pierre Mesnard. Vol. V, 3 of Corpus général des philosophes français. Paris, 1951.

—— Six livres de la république. 4th ed. Paris, 1579.

—— La Response de Jean Bodin à M. Malestroit 1568, ed. Henri Hauser. Paris, 1932.

Budé (Budaeus), Guillaume. Annotationes Gulielmi Budaei in quatuor et viginti Pandectarum libros, bound together with Annotationes reliquiae in Pandectas. Paris, 1535.

—— Annotationes reliquae in Pandectas, bound together with Annotationes Gulielmi Budaei in quatuor et viginti Pandectarum libros. Paris, 1535.

Cano, Melchior. Melchioris Cani . . . opera. . . . Bassani, 1776.

Carion, Johann. Chronica Joannis Carionis. Antwerp, 1540.

Chytraeus (Kochaff), David. Chronologia historiae Herodoti et Thucydidis recognita, et additis ecclesiae Christi ac imperii

Romani rebus praecipuis ab initio mundi usque ad nostram aetatem contexta. Rostock, 1573.

Doneau (Donellus), Hugues. Hugonis Donelli opera omnia, ed. O. Hilligerus. Vol. I. Rome, 1828.

Du Moulin (Molinaeus), Charles. De concordia et unione consuetudinum Franciae, in Carolus Molinaeus, Tractatus commerciorum et usarum. Lyons, 1572.

Gentili (Gentilis), Alberico. De iuris interpretibus dialogi sex, ed. Guido Astuti. Turin, 1937.

Hotman (Hotomannus), François. Antitribonianus sive dissertatio de studio legum, in Variorum opuscula ad cultiorem jurisprudentiam adsequendam pertinentia. Vol. VII. Pisa, 1771.

LeRoy (Regius), Louis. De la vicissitude ou varieté des choses en l'univers, sel. G. W. Bates. Princeton, 1944.

Melanchthon, Philipp, and Gaspar Peucer. Chronicon Carionis expositum et auctum multis et veteribus et recentibus historiis. Lyons, 1586.

Pico della Mirandola, Gianfrancesco. Ioannis Francisci Pici opera quae extant omnia, in Opera omnia Ioannis Pici Mirandulae. 2 vols. Basel, 1572–73. (The works of Gianfrancisco Pico della Mirandola constitute volume II.)

Possevino, Antonio. Apparatus ad omnium gentium historiam. Venice, 1597.

Ramus (Ramée), Peter. Petri Rami dialecticae institutiones, in Antonius Goveanus, Opera. Rotterdam, 1766.

Valla, Lorenzo. De falso credita et ementita Constantini Donatione declamatio, ed. Walther Schwahn. Leipzig, 1928.

Vives, Juan Luis. Opero omnia. Vols. II, VI. Valencia, 1782–90.

II. OTHER WORKS

Allen, J. W. A History of Political Thought in the Sixteenth Century. London, 1957.

Astuti, Guido. Mos italicus e mos gallicus nei dialoghi, "De Iuris Interpretibus" di Alberico Gentili. Bologna, 1937.

Aubépin, M. "De l'influence de Dumoulin sur la législation française," Revue critique de législation et de jurisprudence, III (1852–53), 608–25.

Augustine, St. (Aurelius Augustinus). Fathers of the Church: Writings of Saint Augustine, Vol. II. New York, 1947.

Baron, J. Franz Hotmann's Antitribonian, ein Beitrag zu den Codificationsbestrebungen vom XVI. bis zum XVIII. Jahrhundert. Berne, 1888.

Baudrillart, Henri. Jean Bodin et son temps. Paris, 1853.

Bernheim, Ernst. Lehrbuch der historischen Methode und der Geschichtsphilosophie. 5th ed. Leipzig, 1908.

Besta, Enrico. L'Opera d'Irnerio. 2 vols. Turin, 1896.

Bezold, Friedrich von. Aus Mittelalter and Renaissance. Munich and Berlin, 1918.

Bloch, Marc. The Historian's Craft. New York, 1953.

Brown, John L. The Methodus ad Facilem Historiarum Cognitionem of Jean Bodin: a Critical Study. Washington, D. C., 1939.

Bury, J. B. The Ancient Greek Historians. New York, 1958.

—— The Idea of Progress. New York, 1955.

Chauviré, Roger. Jean Bodin, auteur de la République. La Flèche, 1941.

Church, William Farr. Constitutional Thought in Sixteenth-Century France. Cambridge, Mass., 1941.

Cicero. De oratore, ed. and trans. E. W. Sutton and H. Rackham. Cambridge, Mass., and London, 1942.

Congar, M-J. "Théologie," in Dictionnaire de théologie catholique (v. 1– , 1909–), XV, 342–502.

Coulton, G. G. Medieval panorama. Cambridge, 1938; New York, 1944.

Declareuil, J. Histoire générale du droit français. Paris, 1925.

Delaruelle, Louis. Guillaume Budé, les origines, les débuts, les idées maîtresses, Paris, 1907.

Engelmann, Woldemar. Die Wiedergeburt der Rechtskultur in Italien. Leipzig, 1939.

Esmein, Adhémar. Cours élémentaire d'histoire du droit français. 15th ed. Paris, 1925.

Eysell, M. A. P. Th. Doneau, sa vie et ses ouvrages. Dijon, 1860.

Ferguson, Wallace R. The Renaissance in Historical Thought. Cambridge, Mass., 1948.

Fineti, L. Palazzini. Storia della ricerca delle interpolazioni nel Corpus Juris Giustineaneo. Milan, 1953.

158 BIBLIOGRAPHY

Flint, Robert. History of the Philosophy of History in France and French Belgium and Switzerland. Edinburgh and London, 1893.

Fournol, E. "Sur quelques traités de droit public au XVIe siècle," *Nouvelle revue historique de droit français et étranger* (3d series) XXI (1897), 298–325.

Freeman, E. A. Introduction to The History of Rome by Theodor Mommsen. London and New York, Everyman, n. d.

Fueter, Eduard. Geschichte der neueren Historiographie. Munich and Berlin, 1911.

Gardeil, A. "Lieux théologiques," in Dictionnaire de théologie catholique, IX, 713–47.

Gilbert, Neal W. Renaissance Concepts of Method. New York, 1960.

Gillot, Hubert. La querelle des anciens et des modernes en France. Paris, 1914.

Hume, David. An Inquiry Concerning Human Understanding. New York, 1955.

Jacquin, M. "Melchior Cano et la théologie moderne," *Revue des sciences philosophiques et théologiques*, IX (1920), 121–41.

Joachimsen, Paul. Geschichtsauffassung und Geschichtsschreibung in Deutschland unter dem Einfluss des Humanismus. Leipzig and Berlin, 1910.

Jolowicz, H. F. Historical Introduction to the Study of Roman Law. 2d ed. Cambridge, 1952.

Kan, Joseph van. Les efforts de codification en France. Paris, 1929.

Kantorowicz, Hermann. Studies in the Glossators of the Roman Law. Cambridge, 1938.

Kisch, Guido. Humanismus und Jurisprudenz, der Kampf zwischen mos italicus und mos gallicus an der Universität Basel. Basel, 1955.

Koschaker, Paul. Europa und das römische Recht. Munich and Berlin, 1953.

Kristeller, Paul Oskar. Renaissance Thought. New York, 1961.

Kuypers, F. "Vives in seiner Pädagogik," *Neue Jahrbücher für Philologie und Pädagogik*, CLVI (1897), 1–36.

Lamprecht, Franz. Zur Theorie der humanistische Geschichts-schreibung, Mensch und Geschichte bei Francesco Patrizzi. Zurich, 1950.

Lang, Albert. Die Loci Theologici des Melchior Cano und die Methode des dogmatischen Beweises. Münchener Studien zur historischen Theologie, Vol. 6. Munich, 1925.

Langlois, C. V., and C. Seignobos. Introduction to the Study of History, trans. G. Perry. New York, 1898.

Lenglet du Fresnoy, N. A New Method of Studying History. 2 vols. London, 1730.

McRae, Kenneth D. "Ramist Tendencies in the Work of Jean Bodin," *Journal of the History of Ideas*, XVI (1955), 306–25.

Maffei, Domenico. Gli Inizi dell'umanesimo giuridico. Milan, 1956.

Maffei, Enrico. Trattati dell'arte storica dal rinascimento fino al secolo XVII. Naples, 1897.

Menke-Gluckert, Emil. Die Geschichtsschreibung der Reformation und Gegenreformation. Leipzig, 1912.

Mesnard, Pierre. L'essor de la philosophie politique au XVIe siècle. 2d. ed. Paris, 1951.

—— "Introduction à la Méthode de l'histoire de Jean Bodin." Bibliothèque d'humanisme et renaissance, travaux et documents, XII (1950), 318–23.

—— "Jean Bodin à Toulouse." Bibliothèque d'humanisme et renaissance, travaux et documents, XII (1950), 31–59.

—— "La place de Cujas dans la querelle de l'humanisme juridique," *Revue historique de droit français et étranger*, 4th ser., 28th yr. (1950, no. 4), pp. 521–37.

Meuten, Anton. Bodins Theorie von der Beeinflussung des politischen Lebens der Staaten durch ihre geographische Lage. Bonn, 1904.

Moreau-Reibel, Jean. Jean Bodin et le droit publique comparé dans ses rapports avec la philosophie de l'histoire. Paris, 1933.

Naef, Henri. "La jeunesse de Bodin, ou les conversions oubliées." Bibliothèque d'humanisme et renaissance, travaux et documents, VIII (1946), 521–37.

Phillipson, Coleman. "Andrea Alciati and His Predecessors," in Great Jurists of the World: Continental Legal History Series, vol. II. Boston, 1914.

—— "Jacques Cujas," in Great Jurists of the World: Continental Legal History Series, vol. II. Boston, 1914.

Pocock, J. G. A. The Ancient Constitution and the Feudal Law. Cambridge, 1957.

Polman, Pontien. L'Élément historique dans la controverse religieuse de XVIe siècle. Grembloux, 1932.

Polybius. Histories, trans. E. S. Shuckburgh. 2 vols. London, 1889.

Quintilian, M. Fabi Quintiliani Institutionis oratoriae liber decimus, ed. W. P. Peterson. London, 1891.

Renz, Fritz. Jean Bodin, ein Beitrag zur Geschichte der historischen Methode im 16. Jahrhundert. Gotha, 1905.

Reynolds, Beatrice. "Shifting Currents in Historical Criticism," *Journal of the History of Ideas*, XIV (1953), 471–92.

Savigny, Friedrich Carl von. Geschichte des römischen Rechts im Mittelalter. 6 vols. Heidelberg, 1815–31.

Schulz, Fritz. History of Roman Legal Science. Oxford, 1953.

Sextus Empiricus. Against the Professors. Cambridge, Mass., and London, 1949.

Shotwell, James T. The History of History. New York. 1939.

Smith, Munroe. The Development of European Law. New York, 1928.

Stintzing, R. Geschichte der deutschen Rechtswissenschaft, Vol. I. Munich and Leipzig, 1880.

Tooley, M. J. Introduction to Six Books of the Commonwealth by Jean Bodin, trans. and sel. by M. J. Tooley. New York, 1955.

Vinogradoff, Paul. Roman Law in Medieval Europe. 2d ed. Oxford, 1929.

Woolf, Cecil N. S. Bartolus of Sassoferrato. Cambridge, 1913.

INDEX

Absolutism, moderate, 42n
Accursius: *glossa ordinaria* of, 11; errors in, discovered by Guillaume Budé, 21, 22
Agnellus, Bishop of Ravenna, 93n
Agricola, Rodolphus, 105n
Agrippa, Henry Cornelius, 89–96
Alciato, Andrea, 26
Annals, 91, 98, 115, 122–23, 130–31, 136
Annius of Viterbo, 121–26 *passim*
Annotationes in Pandectas (Budé), 18–25
Antitribonianus (Hotman), 46–58
Archives, 136n; *see also* Annals
Augustine, St., 108 and n, 109n

Barbarossa (Frederick I), 8n
Bartolism, 12–17, 64–65
Bartolus of Sassoferrato, 12–17 *passim*
Baudouin, François: and methodology of history, 3–4; proposals for universally based jurisprudence, 36–37, 42–46; on historical methodology, 116–36
Bloch, Marc, quoted, 101–2n
Bodin, Jean: and reconstruction of juristic science, 2–4; and methodology of history, 3–4; on jurisprudence versus humanist studies, 25n, 61–63; proposals for universally based jurisprudence, 36–37, 67–79; religious views, 40n; comparative approach to universal jurisprudence, 59–79; on Jacques Cujas, 64; on historical methodology, 137–54
Bologna law school, 7–8
Brocardica, 10
Budé, Guillaume, and jurisprudence, 18–26

Cano, Melchior, on historical methodology, 103–15
Chytraeus (Kochaff), David, 124–25
Cicero, 134–35 and nn
Codex Pisanus (*Littera Florentina*), 20
Commentarii de Jure Civili (Doneau), 31–35
Comparison, process of, in Bodin, 76–77
Connan, François, 30
Corpus Juris, standard medieval edition of, 8; *see also* Roman Law
Coulton, G. G., on medieval historical method, 93n
Cujas, Jacques, 26, 60–61, 64
Customary laws, in France, 37 ff.

Declareuil, J., on medieval jurisprudence, 39n
De historia dialogi X (Patrizzi), 97–102